SAINT PAUL'S SCHUBERT CLUB:
A CENTURY OF MUSIC
(1882 - 1982)

This book is dedicated
to
Miss Ethelwyn Power

and the memory of
Miss Margaret MacLaren
and
Miss Elizabeth Dorsey

Saint Paul's Schubert Club:
A Century of Music
(1882~1982)

by

James Taylor Dunn

THE SCHUBERT CLUB
SAINT PAUL, MINNESOTA

Library of Congress Catalog Card Number 83-061 091

ISBN 0-912373-02-4

Published by
North Central Publishing Company
©1983 by The Schubert Club
St. Paul, Minnesota 55102
All Rights Reserved
October, 1983

CONTENTS

(x)

(x)

PREFACE

Tradition and continuity are important. Some of a person's deepest needs are met, as Edith Wharton wrote in a little book in 1908, by "keeping intact as many links as possible between yesterday and tomorrow."

The Schubert Club's roots reach far back into the beginnings of Saint Paul. Governor Alexander Ramsey's daughter Marion Furness, as well as Margaret MacLaren, Elizabeth Dorsey and Ethelwyn Power (currently our Assistant Treasurer), have each spent over fifty years on the Schubert Club Board of Directors. Programs such as the student scholarship awards have existed for over sixty years. The Schubert Club Keyboard Instrument Museum contains instruments, including several Italian harpsichords, which date back three and four hundred years. And the Schubert Club offices and Museum are fittingly ensconced in the handsome old Landmark Center.

We take a measure of pride in our tradition and are deeply grateful to James Taylor Dunn for once again writing a monograph on the history of the Schubert Club and to Patricia Hampl for her beautiful introduction.

— Bruce Carlson
Executive Director

INTRODUCTION

THE RECITAL: A REFLECTION

It wasn't raining — that much I remember — when I stepped outside. An April morning in 1957, maybe '58. The sky must have been threatening, but I didn't notice. No doubt I was in that heaven of relief, that transcendence of escape, which claimed me every Saturday when, having walked along the dim gold corridor past Sister Portress who was crippled and bent double like a benign crone in an old tale, I opened first the inner grille and then the outer green door, and emerged from the Visitation Convent onto Fairmount Avenue, leaving behind on the fourth floor, with its many heavy pianos, the still heavier hour of my weekly piano lesson. That unfortunate hour.

Unfortunate maybe especially for Sister Mary Louise, who was my teacher. Or for the housewifely nuns peacefully cleaning and scrubbing their classrooms in the lovely Saturday silence, a silence broken raggedly by me. (I was the only Saturday student, sent over from my own grade school, St. Luke's, "for piano" as if for a cup of borrowed sugar.) Or sometimes, I thought it was the very hallways which I disturbed, those cool, shadowy monastery avenues with their rows of class portraits bearing the unblemished faces of studio photography dating from early in the century.

These photographs were mounted above eye level (well, I was only 11 or 12). Their lambent, air-brushed radiance was not of graduation pictures but of the girl saints stamped in ovals on holy cards, intended for veneration. They were iconic, those serene graduates of the past, their floating heads unperturbed by the rising mist (it looked like) that had enveloped them to the shoulders and — who could say? — might rise still further and extinguish them absolutely. Their disregard bespoke an ease never to be mine — I knew it — in life or in art.

The art in question at the moment was music: the heavy furniture on the fourth floor. When I arrived at her studio Sister Mary Louise was already there, waiting for me. She would be dusting the grand piano which was placed at an angle in the large, attractively disordered room. Sheet music everywhere in piles; a bust of Schubert, one of Chopin, both done in some salt-white stone; on the window sills, glasses and jars filled with the soupy water you see in aquariums, but here used to root the cuttings Sister had taken from plants. She was always encouraging some twig or leaf on her window sill. She used one of those poufy dusters made of soft feathers on the big piano, wisking it over wood and keyboard. Grooming the beast.

To be clear: I loved the piano, both this one with its black bulk and surprisingly easy, pliant action (a piano rumored to be the property of the archbishop himself), and any piano, that instrument which, to my ear, has always seemed to have a beautiful distant bell sounding somewhere in the tension of felt and wire. I loved too the deep privacy of the empty building, the Saturday silence, the French monastic feel of the old place which seemed more arty than religious. And I loved Sister Mary Louise.

Maybe the kinesthetic nature of piano playing creates a special bond between teacher and student. It was unique in my experience, but student athletes may have a similar feeling for the tennis coach or the swimming coach. For one thing, there was only so much Sister Mary Louise could *tell* me. The hands, the little stupid hands, had to get smart in their own sweet mind-body time. We both understood this, and Sister, patient beyond reckoning, respected even the sullen slowness of those hands. It was a mutual, almost comradely relation, fluid and respectful as I liked to suppose all personal encounters were in the aristocracy of adulthood.

The impersonal nature of the discipline was liberating. We were studying quality, not only music. How pleasant to have the undivided attention of an adult whose focus was not on me, but on my hands. A small distinction perhaps, but it created a nice detachment, one children are rarely given.

Sister Mary Louise and I were not simply teacher and student; we were united in endeavor, tethered to each other as climbers are by bright nylon, going up a sheer face by inches. We were separate, alone —yet we needed each other. Or I needed her. I didn't mind needing her; it didn't seem childish.

Yet all was not well up there on the fourth floor in the airy studio whose windows were set high, giving a view of much sky and the aimless, feathery tops of old spreading elms that swayed or lurched or stood perfectly still, depending on the weather. The problem, simply outlined, was: A) I had no talent; B) I didn't practise. Which just about took care of all the chances Sister Mary Louise had to make something of me.

I could not sight-read. As for playing "by ear" — I hadn't even figured out "Chop-sticks," and had learned it, laboriously, from a neighbor boy. If I hoped to imitate the elegant nonchalance of Walter Gieseking and Robert Casadesus as they dipped their deft oars through the glassy waters of Debussy and Ravel on the monaural records Sister played for me, then I had first to slog my way through the impassable marshes and weedy lagoons of the ungifted. I had to practise. Hard. Scales, arpeggios, measure one, measure two, on an on, doggedly building the little architecture of each piece like an unremarkable house I was grateful to have, be it ever so humble. The modesty of hard work. Practise, daily practise.

But this, listening to the effortless, urbanely light playing of Robert Casadesus, I was not prepared to undertake. Sister slid the record out of its album, wiped it swiftly with a soft white cloth she had for the purpose, and laid it on the turntable, bending down to place the needle immaculately on target. The low sloshing sound between bands provided a brief overture while Sister reminded me to notice the stern *legato* of Robert Casadesus: "There's more *legato* to Debussy than people realize. That's why," she said gently, not for the first time, "it's important to count, dear."

But I did not attend to Robert Casadesus's *legato*, and I did not count. The metronome drove me wild with its mean-spirited persistence, especially Sister's new electric one which hadn't even the kindness to wind down and become exhausted. True, Sister rarely tortured me with the metronome, but the matter of counting seemed never long from her thoughts.

What was I listening to, then, while Sister patted the air before her in a *tableau vivant* of the well-counted *legato* line and Robert Casadesus went rippling on, oar in, oar out, hardly breaking the surface as he moved forward? The truth is, I wasn't listening at all. I was looking.

Or rather, I was *seeing*, the milky fascinated seeing of pure (that is, wicked) fantasy. I was seeing Robert Casadesus . . . In Recital.

From there it was a small hop to seeing myself . . . In Recital. Myself triumphant. The piano, all of the piano literature drifted behind, becoming a sort of rag-tag retinue to the sovereign, spot-lighted me.

Sister, I never heard a note. I was long gone from the fourth floor studio, from the archbishop's piano, from the damp, just-blotted sound of the monaural Debussy, from every good intention you thought we shared about the value of counting aloud. Gone from the morning, gone from the monastery. I was in the glittery evening, dressed to kill (strange phrase, so feminine in its acuity), entering, alone, the recital hall, the arena of solitary per-formance where I imagined skill and character need not be won, but merely displayed.

And that is why, loving the piano and also Sister Mary Louise and her patient ways, I still felt a relieved jolt of escape when I left my lesson on the fourth floor and regained the street. There was a lie being told up there, a lie in the form of inattention and sloth. And even a liar hates a lie.

Pointless for Sister to inquire kindly about my school work and "other duties and chores" in an effort to help me "organize my practise time." There is no organizing a day-dreamer, that person intent on perfecting the versions of fantasy. I had no time to practise— I needed every moment to *play* the piano, to perform.

So it was at home, where I spent hours banging away for my audience of naught. I have known the exhaustion of the solo performer, there in our living room, playing for my-self (that is, for the world.) I was dead to discipline, alive only to the impish daimon of the daydream.

But the Saturday I'm thinking of, the one in April when I didn't notice the gathering storm, was special. I was brought out of the daydream (or into a new one) while still on the fourth floor, sitting with Sister at the big piano, ringed by her jars of would-be plants. It was one of the days, which came only twice or three times a year, when Sister presented me with my new sheet music, the new pieces we were to study for the coming months.

April, a general dampness in the air, the swollen beginnings of Spring, the edgiest time of year, though the habit is to think of Spring as hopeful. Anyway, Spring, and here I was, given a double reprieve: not only the usual escape from the trusting Sister after yet another week when I had not practised, but the rarer release into new, untried music. Like all those elderly cuttings on Sister's window sill, I could turn over a new leaf. Begin again, start afresh — all those middle-aged hopes were mine at age twelve as I got on my blue Raleigh to glide away, leaving the red brick of the heavy convent behind.

I could not have handled the thin cream paper of the flimsy Editions Gallimard, more tenderly if they had been expensive shirts hand-finished at a French laundry. The un-translated French titles, literary as if they named short stories rather than music, were ap-pealing too. Sister Mary Louise had repeated them in French several times so that I, know-ing no French, could learn them by rote: "La fille aux cheveux de lin," "La cathedrale engloutee." Who was this girl with flaxen hair, and what, exactly, was an engulfed cathe-dral? It didn't matter — I sensed the mystery of these images, I absorbed them: they were France and music and the stately barge of Robert Casadesus. And they were snugly in my free hand, as I rode my bicycle single-handed up Fairmount Avenue toward home.

Toward home and serious work. *This* time, this time I would practise. I would study. I would forego the immediate ecstasy, and hold out for the sterner stuff of Casadesus. Like him and Walter Gieseking (whose rendition of Mendelssohn's *Song without Words* Sister had counted out for me), I would row, row, row my boat gently up the measured stream.

It was not too late! There was still time! Here I was with the perfect, fresh cream sheet music, sailing nicely along the creosote block paving of Fairmount which chattered companionably whenever a car passed over it, and wasn't life grand?

It was a set-up. I see that now.

The rain hit before I reached the cross-street of Milton, hardly halfway home. It came at first in long, careless strokes. The sort of incidental gesture it is possible to ignore, to imagine away. But not for long. Those dabs fast became a deluge. I panicked, all afright for the delicate rolled *crepes* of my French music, engulfed indeed.

This must not happen: the iron thought rose not out of my mind but straight from my breast-bone. I brought the bike to a stop at the corner of Milton, pulled up my blouse and undershirt, thrust the sheets, unrolled, next to my skin, and covered up. And panted for a moment, getting my bearings.

Back on the bicycle. Raining very hard now — how had I not seen that evil gathering in the sky; how had Sister not noticed. But what can you expect, I thought disloyally, from a cloistered nun in the way of an outdoor matter like the weather.

It was raining now in a mad fit. It would rain forever. Get home fast — that was the only thing to do.

But as soon as I was back on the bike, I saw I was sunk. Death by drowning I had avoided, but now, clutching my chest to hold the music in place like a bandage over a mortal wound, I realized I would perish by wrinkling. The whole point was to safeguard that perfect, smooth cream paper, that France of music, the impressionistic soul of my daydream. I was ruining the thing by trying to save it.

Off the bike again, holding one hand lightly to my chest, the other extended to balance the bike. Soon, if I didn't think of something, I would be drowning again: my jacket was already sodden. Life narrowed to the two choices, and in an anguish of inde-cision, I became a failure at existential choice before I'd finished grade school.

I stood on the corner of Milton and Fairmount and sobbed, just sobbed. I had no plan, I was without hope (Hope, that last trouble to waft out of Pandora's box).

Who can say why a certain moment, one frail incident of no special value in itself, becomes the riveted center of a symbol? Why do certain episodes become meaningful be-yond themselves, and others remain only what they are, bright as dandelions for a moment and then blown away without a shred of significance left? Why do we remember this, and not the other?

But it happens; a gilt frame goes around a certain moment, and the picture hangs forever in the history of personality. The gold frame went around that sedgy day, taking in April and the caged leaves just reaching their twisted hands out of the sheath of buds; taking in the slick street, where that small person stood, hand on heart, sobbing aloud next to a blue bicycle.

I needed a miracle — which is something altogether different from a daydream. Maybe that is why the moment is framed so conclusively, why it keeps returning. I held my daydream close to my heart — and still I could do nothing to save it. The magical, unreal recitals of the mind must really, truly end. There is such a thing as a real world: full of rain and other tough disciplines. *This* was what I must contend with, where I must live.

Maybe I make too much of the moment. If I do, still, that's the way it was, even as I stood there, and the firm gold frame was forming around me and the instant, making its permanent picture with the inevitable title: The Crossroads.

As for the real recitals I had played in, those kiddy phantasmagoria of stage-fright — they were death by fire. Sister was always surprised that I was more nervous than any of the other girls when an actual recital came around. And she had wondered when I declined the chance to compete in the Schubert Club piano competitions for children. It must have seemed strange to her, for of course she knew I was a ham.

But the big-time life of the daydream allows for no interruption by the small-fry of reality. Forget the peanut gallery of Mother and Dad, brother and friends. Once faced with a real recital, I was unable to detach from the daydream long enough to understand fully where I was: St. Paul, Minnesota, a small auditorium in a small school, surrounded by indulgent family. I was . . . well, probably in Paris, certainly at least in New York. And there was Robert Casadesus in the front row, fanning himself with the mimeoed program, a man not to be fooled. I only got through those recitals by letting out one-tenth of the *brio* I indulged at home, playing for my airy audience.

Standing on the corner in the driving rain, soaked to the skin (I almost wrote, soaked to the soul), I think I knew — or I felt — that the absolute reverie of accomplishment by daydream was at an end. I couldn't think my way out of this.

I stood there crying, just waiting for ruin, for the impressionistic music of France which I loved (daydream music, that) to be reclaimed by water, its true element.

And then, on cue, the miracle came, once I'd given up.

I suppose, for me, an archangel will always immediately bring to mind a middle-aged man in a taupe fedora, a concerned face leaning out of a car window in a driving rain. There was another angel, a woman I think, in the seat next to him.

I could hardly speak when he asked what the trouble was; I was convulsed by sobs. Or maybe a daydreamer is one who doesn't fully believe in the existence of other people, in their ability to help. I hardly understood he could save the situation.

But he somehow got the message across and made a plan. I handed over the still salvagable sheet music (bent but not wrinkled), and he agreed to deliver it to my house, to my mother. This left me free to ride home on my bike, happy as a jay in the rain. For getting myself wet was a joy, a baptism.

Never mind that my mother, seeing the taupe fedora coming up the front steps holding a sheaf of piano music ("All that was left of you, I thought when I saw that man"), immediately assumed that I was dead. Never mind that she could not comprehend the soul-anguish of The Crossroads ("Why didn't you just pedal home?"). I knew I had been saved.

The daydream, however, did not survive. All to the good. Oh, there were moments — still are — playing *Clair de lune* or the first movement of the "Moonlight Sonata" (the only movement of the sonata I attempt) when a sedate, definitely *andante* charisma comes over me and I'm on stage again, my vast ghostly audience rapt, paying homage in their spooky way to my counterfeit gift. Such brief egomania harms nobody, I figure, not even me. And certainly not the music which is beyond any harm or good I could ever do it. Music survived the crossroads too.

Thinking of that moment when I lost a good deal (never underestimate the despair of childhood) on the corner of Milton and Fairmount, and when I was given, by a compassionate stranger, something I hadn't known I required, I wonder if something else did not become symbolic that day. The gold frame that rings that episode with significance for me seems also to have etched itself around the very art form I was pursuing. Music, yes. But beyond music (or rather, within it) the form of the recital, that purest, most unadorned mode of musical performance. The personal form, the most nearly essential. And most defenseless.

What does it mean to walk, solo, onto a stage, some piece of wood or metal or simply your own vocal cords for your companion? No hiding. No howling for help if a rainy street corner gets the better of you. Just: the self, the stage, the world, the waiting world. For in *this* recital hall (the real one of the real artist) the daydream comes true: the audience seated in its chairs does become the world. It stands for the world. That's how symbols work.

And the musician, like an earnest school child, does "say his piece," does *recite*, as if in the very word chosen for the form, we understand that to stand alone, to be an artist performing without the cover of props or costume or cunning stagecraft, is somehow to *speak*, to make articulate what before was held inchoate and therefore lost within the heart. To speak in music, language past language, one disarmed being calling to (or, really, *for*) the rest of us.

And isn't that — the solo artist standing before us — as useful a symbol as any for what we each must do as we go about our daily business, dodging the mean rain, or facing it head on?

—Patricia Hampl

I. MUSIC ON THE FRONTIER

First the military and then the explorers brought into the vastness of
what later became Minnesota the beginnings of a high standard of culture and
a rich heritage of music. Life on the frontier, therefore, was not entirely one
of drudgery and unceasing toil. Almost from the beginning the soothing
sounds of music occasionally helped allay the problems of pioneer living.

In 1824, for example, when Captain Joseph Plympton arrived at Fort
Snelling with his bride, a treasured piano accompanied them into the wilder-
ness. During the late 1830s the distinguished French scientist and explorer-
surveyor, Joseph N. Nicollet, on assignment to survey the region between the
Mississippi and Missouri rivers, was the guest of Lawrence Taliaferro, Indian
agent at the fort.   Taliaferro later recorded in his autobiography that "for
hours each night" Nicollet's accomplishments on the violin, to the accompaniment of Mrs. Taliaferro's piano, helped pass two "long and dreary" winters at
lonely Fort Snelling. There must have been other similar, yet unrecorded, in-
cidences.

A decade later the pioneer settlers in nearby St. Paul also brought
with them from Europe and the eastern seaboard a refinement they wished
to continue in the new region.

"I cannot imagine a finer society than existed in the village of Mendota,
St. Paul, and St. Anthony, and at Fort Snelling, small as the numbers were."
These were the words of Rebecca Marshall, later Mrs. Alexander H. Cathcart,
the sister of future Minnesota governor William R. Marshall. As an elderly dow-
ager, Mrs. Cathcart recalled life in territorial Minnesota in a reminiscent talk
given before the Minnesota Historical Society in 1913. She specially singled
out one settler who added much to the gaiety and social life of St. Paul after
arriving in 1849. He was Danish-born Charles W. W. Borup, a former fur trader,
a skilled musician, and founder of a pioneer St. Paul banking firm. His home
was, according to several early accounts, "The center and inspiration" of local
musical activities. There were others, too, who added luster to this elite coterie
of music afficionados: Borup's business partner and brother-in-law Charles H.
Oakes; Mrs. Ignatius Donnelly, wife of the feisty Minnesota politician, and Mrs.
Isaac Ven Etten, Borup's niece; both had "very lovely flexible voices"; and
Mrs. Henry M. Knox, wife of a St. Paul banker, who as Charlotte Cozzins was
trained for opera, but gave up her career for marriage to become locally popular as "the most charming of ballad singers."

Back in 1849, however, when Minnesota became a territory and newly appointed governor Alexander Ramsey arrived here from the East with his family, he and his peers could see only a dozen frame houses and a few log buildings. Nevertheless, these were the crude dwellings that sheltered the beginnings of a musical consciousness in Minnesota. It was at Ramsey's first home, a humble predecessor of his elegant 1872 Exchange Street house, that a quiet little girl, from her "seat of vantage in the corner of the parlor sofa," sat "watching and listening" to the musicians, "divided between delight at this new experience and dread of eternally disgracing myself by falling asleep and having to be carried off to bed." That little girl was Ramsey's daughter Marion who will later play an important role in this story. Music had indeed become a part of frontier St. Paul home life as early as people had time to enjoy it.

By the later 1850s and into the 1860s, musical activities burgeoned in this area and in other Minnesota towns. There was a growing public interest in the individual performer, and as a result recitalists and touring groups, braving the rigors of travel, hit the waterways and whatever roads existed to bring music and theater to the hinterland of America. One of the earliest to visit Minnesota was the great Norwegian violin virtuoso Ole Bull who in July, 1856, gave two joint recitals in the state (one in St. Paul and the other in Stillwater) with the thirteen-year-old singer Adelina Patti who later became the most famous coloratura soprano of her day. While St. Paul critics enthusiastically praised her, and a St. Anthony reviewer commented mildly, "She is not a singer yet," St. Croix Valley listeners felt that her untrained voice was little more than endurable. Ole Bull, however, was received with unstinted enthusiasm.

Throughout the years of music development in early St. Paul, one name stood out above the others. It was that of Richards Gordon, local furrier, who accomplished much on behalf of musical societies. Gordon, stated a contemporary, "probably did more than any one man to make St. Paul a musical city." Richards Gordon and Charles Borup (mentioned above) are grandfather and great-grandfather by marriage of the present Mrs. C. Richards Gordon, a Schubert Club board member active in music therapy.

By 1872 several all-male German singing societies like the St. Paul Liederkranz had been organized, and regular public concerts continued to be presented in Ingersoll's Hall at Bridge Square by the St. Paul Musical Society orchestra. It was a recent outgrowth of a quartet of string players — Gustav Hancke, Herman Macklett, Conrad Zenzius, and George Seibert — who enjoyed playing together informally for their friends and their own entertainment. The group soon became perhaps the best-known early orchestral organization of St. Paul and survived for a quarter of a century as one of the leading instrumental ensembles in the state.

In April, 1872, Joseph Haven Hanson, clerk at the Munger Brothers music store in St. Paul, boasted in the first issue of a local literary journal, *The Busy West*, that there was "no better way to judge the character of a people, than by their musical attainments." In St. Paul, therefore, he felt that "the musical taste displayed is something wonderful, when we consider our extreme youth."

Participation in musical organizations appeared at this time, however, to be limited to men, with only an occasional female soloist taking part. Hanson was not remiss in tempering his enthusiasm by complaining that he found "wretched music in the churches, with few exceptions. Not even a single singing school."

Even as late as 1880 St. Paul still lacked an organized group of men or women dedicated to the presentation in recital of a solo voice or instrument. By this time the informal home musical "soirées" of pioneer days, where families and friends gathered around a piano or melodeon for an evening of music, had changed to all-female "matinees" held at varied locations. These included, among others, the Frederick Driscoll home on Summit Avenue and the Alexander Ramsey residence on Exchange Street where the former governor's daughter Marion, (Mrs. Charles E. Furness) was hostess. The popularity of these events steadily increased so they soon outgrew the crowded parlors and hallways of private homes.

The stage was set.

It was time for the forty or so women who regularly attended these social teas to act. On an afternoon late in 1882 this group of energetic St. Paulites gathered at a Summit Avenue home to form a cohesive group. Little did they know at that time of small beginnings that they would be putting into motion the makings of one of the longest-lived musical organizations in America, one known across the country for its uncompromisingly high standards of music. The soon-to-be-called Schubert Club was off and running and today continues to develop and grow after one hundred years of continuous service as a musical mentor to the Northwest.

༻⊙⊪⊙༺

II. THE BEGINNINGS: 1882 - 1902

It was on May 21, 1882, that the popular author, humorist, and lecturer Mark Twain (real name: Samuel L. Clemens) stopped off at the Metropolitan Hotel on Washington Street in St. Paul and the next day saw the city for the first time. Because of foul weather he remained only one day in this fast-growing capital city of 71,000 persons, but later wrote in *Life on the Mississippi* that "St. Paul's strength lies in her commerce — I mean his commerce. He is a manufacturing city as many of the cities of this region are, but he is particularly strong in commerce . Last year the jobbing trade amounted to $5.2 million."

Twain might have added that St. Paul was becoming a city of culture, too. The St. Paul Public Library was organized in 1882. And before the end of that year the aforementioned women meeting on Summit Avenue — probably at the home of Mrs. Charles McIlrath, wife of the former state auditor—

Franz Schubert, 1797-1828, after whom the "Ladies Musicale" was renamed "The Schubert Club" in 1888.

The Schubert Club trademark was developed by Florence Fairchild (later Mrs. Charles H. Bigelow) in 1892, spelling out "Schubert Club" on the musical staff. It is still in use on most Schubert Club programs.

CONOVER HALL, DEC. 4, 1895.

The Music of the American Indians.

LECTURE, WITH PIANO ILLUSTRATIONS,

— BY —

MISS FRANCES DENSMORE.

..OUTLINE..

SOCIAL SONGS,	Songs of the Hæthuska Society
	Songs of the Poogthun Society
INDIVIDUAL SONGS,	Songs of the Warpath and Battle
	Songs of Love.
RITUAL SONGS,	The Tribal Prayer.
	The Wa-wan, (or Calumet Ceremony)

PROGRAMME.

FEB. 6 - 1890.

I. FOND HEART FAREWELL ______ Hope Temple.
Miss Nellie Fowler.

II. SPANISH DANCES, (op. 12, Nº 2, 3, & 6) ___ Moszkowski.
Mrs. De Celle & Mrs. Fernstrom.

III. THE SHADOWS DEEPEN
ON THE CASTLE WALLS, ______ D. Buck.
(FROM DON MUNIO)
Mr. J. F. Merrill.

IV. { BALLADE, (G. minor) ______ Rheinberger.
{ WIEGENLIED, (Cradle Song.) ______ Kjerulf.
Mrs. H. A. Stahl.

V. OUT ON THE DEEP ______ Löhr.
Mr. J. L. Whelan.

VI. KELLOGG WALTZ ______ Arditi.
Mrs. F. O. Osborne.

Marion Ramsey Furness, President of the Schubert Club in the 1880's, was subsequently elected Vice President for life of the Schubert Club and served on the board until her death in 1935.

Laura Furness, Schubert Club board member, reading to her grandfather Governor Alexander Ramsey on the front porch of the Ramsey House, 265 Exchange Street, St. Paul.

(Upper left and clockwise): Mrs. Julia Dorr, Schubert Club President, 1892-1900; Ella Richards, soprano; Mathilda Heck, St. Paul Public School Music Supervisor 1933-1957; and Elsie Shaw, St. Paul Public School Music Supervisor 1898-1933 and Schubert Club President 1900-1902.

A drawing of Schubert's study in Vienna.

Bockstruck Jewelers store on Fifth Street in downtown St. Paul (along with Frank Murphy across the street) featured instruments from the Schubert Club Keyboard Instrument Museum in window displays during the Schubert Club Centennial Year.

Child prodigees Arma and Margaret Milch at their Schubert Club debut, St. Paul, 1898.

Donald Ferguson, musicologist, composer, annotator, teacher and performer, addressing the Schubert Club's Annual Meeting at the Minnesota Museum of Art on May 14, 1981. Ferguson was introduced with a tribute "Professor Ferguson — 100 Years of Musical Life" by Mary Ann Feldman.

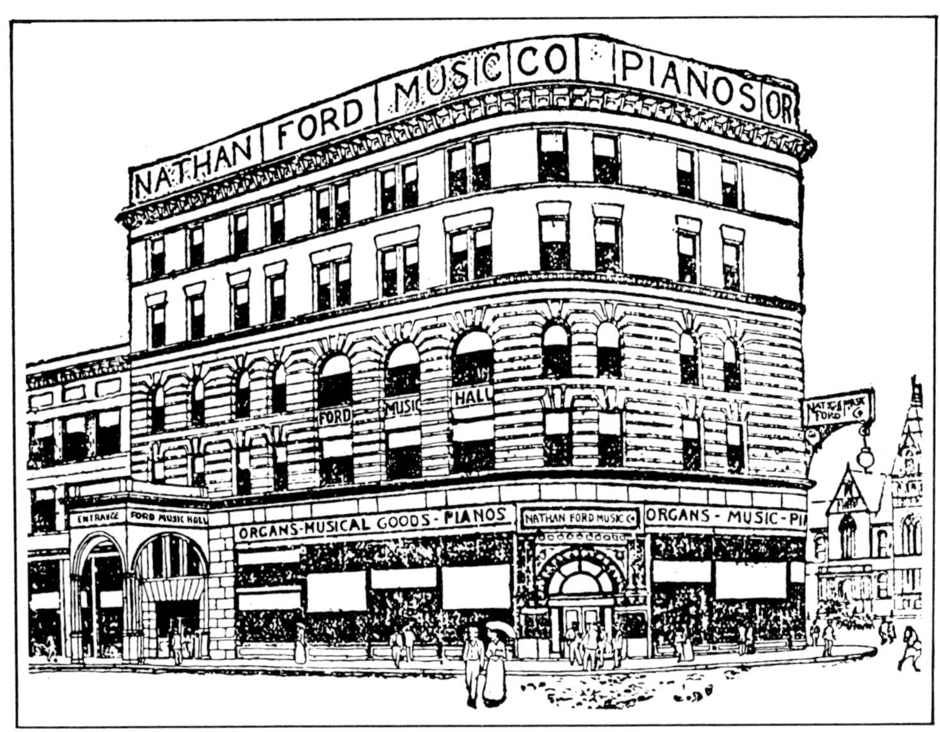

The Ford Music Hall at Sixth and St. Peter streets was a popular location for Schubert Club concerts between 1892 and 1912. This local "Flatiron Building" with a plush third floor auditorium was at various times known as Conover Hall, Raudenbush Hall, the Odeon, the Schiffman Building and the Degree of Honor Building.

The Ford Music Hall was demolished in 1976.

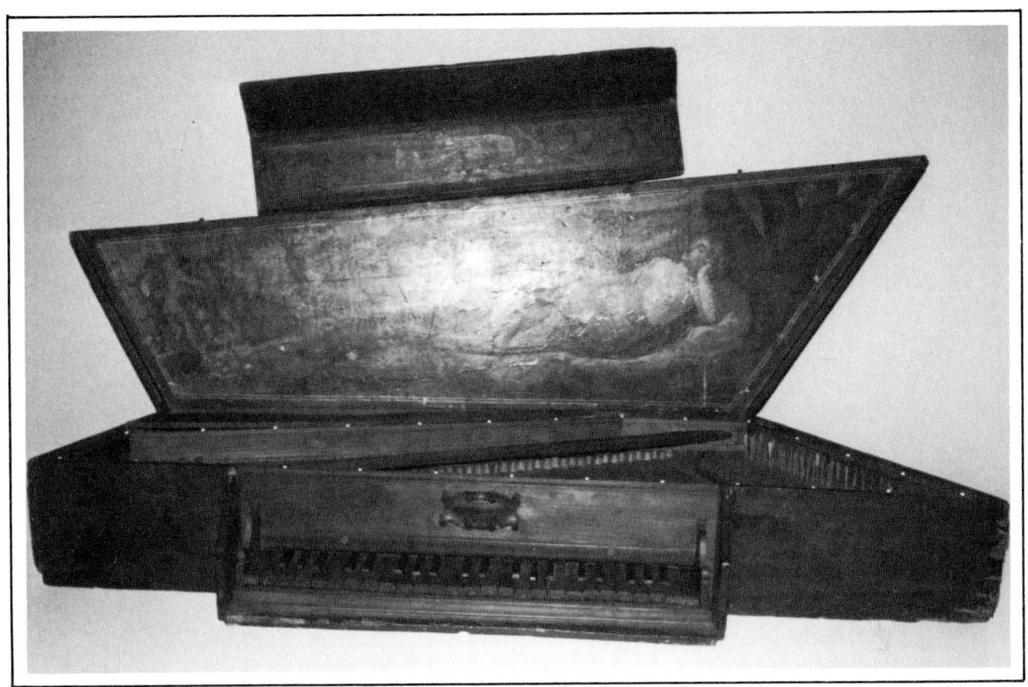

The 1542 Anniable de Rossi harpsichord in the Schubert Club Keyboard Instrument Museum. This is the earliest keyboard instrument by a known maker in the United States. It was secured for the Schubert Club in 1981 by Polly Ordway Wallace.

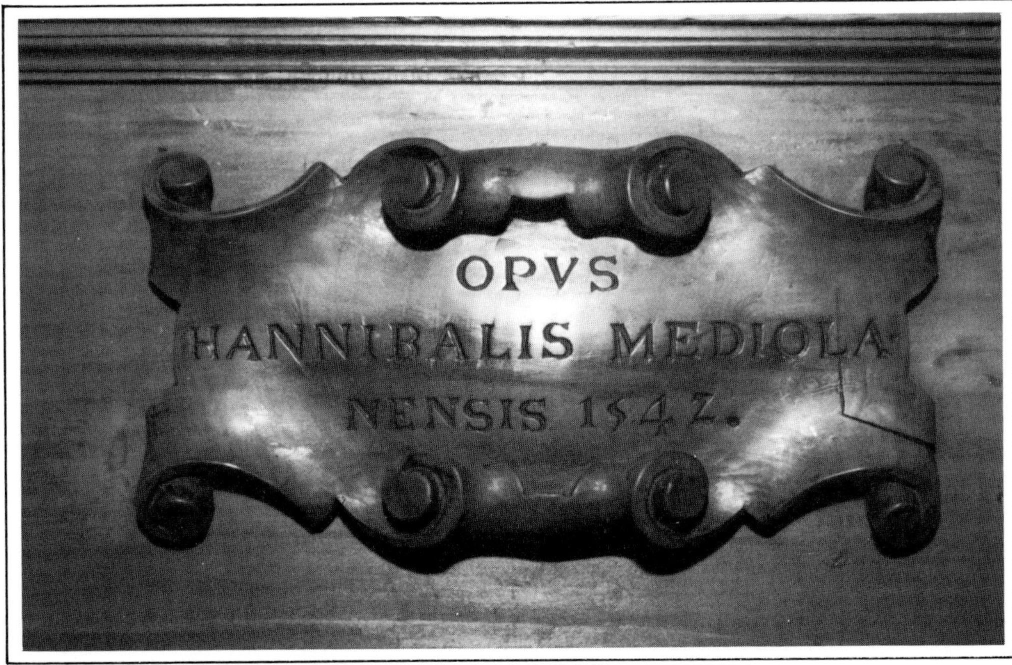

The name plate cartouch on the Anniable de Rossi harpsichord.

An editorial cartoon from the St. Paul *Pioneer Press* in 1908.

Schubert Club International Artists:
(Upper left and clockwise): Eugene Ysäye, violinist, 1895 season; Josef Hofmann, pianist, 1898 season; Fannie Bloomfield Zeisler, pianist, 1901 and 1911 seasons; and Louise Homer, contralto, 1901 and 1913 seasons.

13

organized what was first vaguely called the "Musical Society." Mrs. McIllrath was chosen the group's first president, and a musical committee (later to be known as the executive board) was picked to manage its affairs. Like the pre-1882 gatherings, the first musicales continued to be more social than musical. One member later suggested their informality when she reminisced that "fancy work busied the hands, while musical selections, vocal and instrumental, were rendered by those able and willing to thus afford entertainment."

During 1883 the name of the group was changed to "Ladies Musicale." By 1885, when the club had seventy-five members, its serious purpose was strengthened by dividing memberships into active (musically proficient) and honorary (listening). All were required to pay annual dues pegged at two and five dollars respectively, and prospective active members had to be tested and approved by an examining committee. The meetings were apparently held bi-weekly on Tuesdays from November to April. Club members and local guest artists performed at these functions, many of which continued to be held in private homes.

Among the talented local musicians were such singers as Lewis Shawe, Florence Pace, Harry E. Phillips, David and Elizabeth Colville, Jessica DeWolf, and Katherine Richards Gordon. There were also pianists and accompanists like Mrs. Hermann Sheffer, Samuel Baldwin, Katherine Hoffman, Mathilda Milch, and Ella Richards. Add professional string players —among them Marie Geist Erd, Louis Milch, Emil Straka, Claude Madden, and Arthur Bergh —plus several chamber ensembles like the Beethoven String Quartet that worked assiduously to make chamber music an appreciated art form in Minnesota. All of these local artists, and many more, graced the recital platforms during the earlier years of the Schubert Club.

From 1882 to 1888 at least two women served as club president. They were Mrs. McIlrath and Mrs. Charles E. Furness —Marion Ramsey who lived with her father, the former governor, and her family in their home at Exchange and Walnut streets. When young, Mrs. Furness had studied music in Germany for two years and in 1872, at a benefit concert held in the grand drawing room of the just-built Ramsey house, played Chopin's *Valse Brillante* on the Ramseys' magnificant new Steinway concert grand piano. Although Mrs. Furness served as president of the "Ladies Musicale" for only one season in 1886, she devoted many years as vice-president for life or in some other capacity of supportive usefulness on the board. The advice of this strikingly handsome "grande dame" of quiet dignity, perfect poise, and commanding presence was certainly responsible for a share of the progress of the future Schubert Club. Her daughters, the Misses Laura and Anna Furness, continued the family's interest in the club until their deaths in the 1970s.

The existing historical records for the earliest years of the organization are scant. Many were reported lost when the St. Paul Public Library at Market House burned in 1915, an event which will be returned to later. Recent research shows that, following the presidency of Mrs. Furness, Mrs. Harcourt H. Horn, long prominent in St. Paul's social life, apparently was president for one year, 1887-88. Because of this and other uncertainties, the club decided in 1922, on the eve of a possible birthday, that 1882 should be settled on as its official birthdate. In hesitating over the year, the group acknowledged that its real roots were much more amorphous than that.

During the 1885-86 season, the only one before 1892 for which a complete budget and membership record exists, the club's seventy-five members spent a total of $152. It was early in 1888, during the four-year presidential term of Mrs. Lyman D. Hodge, that the second vacuous name, "Ladies Musicale," was dropped and the organization re-christened the "Schubert Club" to honor famous Austrian composer, Franz Peter Schubert. In short order, the group also adopted its distinctive and familiar logo, a music staff with a clef and notes spelling out the club's name — but musically signifying nothing. Although the exact date of the insignia's first use is not known, it probably was in 1892. The unique sketch, which continues in use today, was the idea of the club's vice-president and social chairman, Florence Fairchild (later Mrs. Charles H. Bigelow), assisted by printer William L. Banning, Jr. During those early years a life-sized bust of Schubert adorned the platform at all meetings and concerts. Although the sculpture has long since vanished, Schubert continued for some years to be honored by occasional memorial concerts, the first of which was apparently given in 1889. After a long span of time Schubert was again honored in 1982, this time with a series of six club centennial lectures concerning "Schubert and His Times."

By the late 1880s the afternoon concerts and study groups were more formally organized. The club adopted what it called a "definite line of musical study" by interspersing its recital programs by active members with lectures and discussions on musical topics. Fortnightly recitals were presented by the actives, and discussions were held on such topics as "The Orchestra," "Dance Forms," and "The Symphony." The talks were usually given with accompaniment.

Addresses on musical subjects were offered not only by club members but by lecturers of national reputation. Among those who traveled to Minnesota was Henry E. Krehbiel, the famed music critic of the *New York Tribune*, who made a number of St. Paul appearances in 1895 to present lectures on drama, Wagner, "Folk-Song in America," and "Dramatic Dances and Children's Games." Minnesota's own Frances Densmore of Red Wing twice that year gave her popular talk, with piano illustrations, about the "Music of the American Indians," and in 1896 New York composer and conductor Walter J. Damrosch lectured in St. Paul on Wagner's "Die Meistersinger" before a delighted audience of Schubert Club members that "taxed the seating capacity of the hall."

Early in the 1892 season, under the presidency of Mrs. Russell R. Dorr, the club adopted a constitution and bylaws, for the first time affirming its aims in print: "To study and practice the best music . . . To advance the interests and promote the culture of musical art in the City of St. Paul." At last St. Paul had an organized group dedicated to recital presentations of local and nationally known vocalists and instrumentalists.

For a few years in the early 1890s an experiment to promote musical art gave local young women a chance to develop their talents. It started as a chorus class for all vocalists "except those . . . prepared to do solo work, when asked." If the recorded rules were followed, the Schubert Club meant business, since it ordered that three unexcused absences from the class would bring expulsion from the club. In 1892 Samuel A. Baldwin, a St. Paul music teacher who was later to become a noted organist and composer, organized a women's chorus from this class. Here was yet another historic shift in Schubert Club activities from the purely private emphasis to a public one. In partial fulfillment of the promise to "promote the culture of musical art," it imported its first prominent artist, bass George E. Holmes, a frequent performer with Theodore Thomas' Chicago Orchestra. Holmes took part with the chorus and other soloists in what was called an excellent performance of Handel's *Messiah* at the People's Church on December 19, 1892. According to the local press, Holmes "easily carried off the honors." The singing of local soprano and active club member Jane Huntington Yale was also "a great delight to the audience." Unfortunately, St. Paul was lax in its support of the efforts of conductor Baldwin. "He deserved better," said the same *St. Paul Pioneer Press* reviewer. On the day following this choral concert, Holmes, assisted by club member pianist Ella Richards, presented a vocal recital at the Christ Church Guild Hall, Fourth and Franklin streets. The program "delighted the ladies present" according to the *St. Paul Pioneer Press* of December 31.

The Schubert Club's first public recital as a series came on March 3, 1893, when German pianist Adele Aus der Ohe performed at Ford Music Hall, "filled from foyer to pit," reported the *Pioneer Press*, "with an assemblage of richly dressed men and women." Also appearing during this first season were violinist Geraldine Morgan, pianist Edward Baxter Perry, and soprano Genevra Johnstone-Bishop. Artistically the 1893 season was a successful foretaste of all the great things to come over the next ninety years.

In 1892 the Schubert Club also evolved into something more than a sanguine group of socialites, many of them friends, who met more or less regularly to enjoy good music. The evolution can trace its beginnings that same year to the start of the eight-year presidency of Mrs. Russell R. Dorr, a gracious, active woman who worked to point the club in a new direction. A former Iowan, an organist by profession who was long identified with the musical life of St. Paul, Julia C. R. Dorr had a definite vision of the Schubert Club as a serious organization which should look outward to the community as well as inward to its membership. She was both a shrewd and tactful administrator endowed with energy and executive ability and a woman of broad cultural contacts, as evidenced by her 1900 election as vice-president and then president of the all-women National Federation of Music Clubs. In these capacities she was the first to urge the acceptance of men into such all-female organizations as the Schubert Club. "In future years," reported *DeLestry's Western Magazine* for February-March, 1898, "when the Schubert Club looks back over the history of its life, it will be with fond memories of Mrs. Dorr's inspiration, influence, and vigorous, untiring assistance." After her departure to live in New York, the *St. Paul Globe* on September 4, 1904, stated that "It does injustice to no one in this city to say that Mrs. Dorr has done more for music here than any other individual. Her thorough technical knowledge, her great executive ability and her enthusiasm were qualities that made her service invaluable." The Schubert Club especially benefitted, for under her strong guidance the club became a real force in St. Paul's cultural life.

Also in 1892 the Schubert Club sought to increase its membership roster, but not at the expense of lowering its standards. The club's active mem-

bers were to be auditioned annually by a committee of accomplished member
artists. Those unable to give satisfactory results could become associates. Re-
quirements for admission to the club were strict, and all aspirants — whether
to active, associate, or honorary status — had to be vouched for by two members and passed on by the board of directors. Today the careful screening of
all musicians who take part in the thirty-nine weekly programs still persists,
and regulations are now only a little altered from those set down in 1892 under
Mrs. Dorr's aegis. As a result of these efforts the membership rose substantially
after 1894, peaked at 430 in 1897, and began declining by 1898. In May, 1901,
it dipped to 203.

During the 1895-96 season the ladies' chorus was raised to new heights
by Elsie M. Shawe who in 1898 became the first supervisor of music in the St.
Paul public school system and for a number of years was its only music teacher.
At the turn of the century she also served a two-year term as club president.
For the 1895-96 season yet another and even more distinguished leader took
over. He was Emil Oberhoffer, a German-born and trained violinist, pianist,
and conductor — a "musical jack-of-all-trades," as Minneapolis critic John K.
Sherman once called him.

Stranded in St. Paul early in the 1890s when a group he was touring
with disbanded, Oberhoffer opened a music school and found additional em-
ployment playing in local restaurants and orchestras. He even published in
New York a pianoforte number called the "Minnesota Boat Club March" to
honor that active St. Paul organization. The Schubert Club soon befriended
him and on several occasions used his services as a lecturer and accompanist.
In late 1897 Oberhoffer was hired as director of the ladies' chorus and its newly
organized orchestra. That was the same year that the club joined a number of
other musical organizations to form the National Federation of Music Club.
Although that group still exists, the Schubert Club dropped its membership in
the 1940s since it was no longer a bona fide "club." The chorus and orchestra
were then open to male participation, and the group was renamed the Schubert
Club Choral Association. The men, however, were refused membership in the
club. In return for a fee of $50 a month, Oberhoffer directed three evening
concerts. Shortly after the turn of the century, however, Minnesota's great
conductor was well on his way to founding the Minneapolis (now Minnesota)
Orchestra. The chorus and orchestra of the Schubert Club did not long survive
his departure, although choral organizations continued to exist in St. Paul.

To present recitals, the club rented a variety of auditoriums at prices
ranging from $3.00 an afternoon to $150 for the season. Among those used
were Litt's Grand Opera House (now replaced by the Garrick Parking Ramp),
Mozart Hall, the former Turnhalle on Franklin Street, and Summit Hall, a building still standing at 512 Laurel Avenue. Some concerts were also held in the
Aberdeen, Ryan, and Windsor hotels, all hostelries of the past, and at the Park
Congregational, Central Presbyterian, and People's churches. But the most
popular location during the first twenty years was the music hall constructed
in 1892 for Nathan Ford, a dealer in musical instruments, and located at the
intersection of Sixth, St. Peter, and Market streets.

After 1895 this local "Flatiron Building" and its once plush, elaborately
decorated third-floor auditorium were known variously as Conover Hall, the

Odeon, Raudenbush Hall, the Schiffman Building, and the Degree of Honor Building. The musical motifs which decorated its St. Peter Street entrance betrayed its original purpose, and the numerous studios in the building at one time or another housed most of St. Paul's best-known musicians and music teachers. The structure was torn down in the 1970s and is today the location of a parking lot.

At least two concerts in the 1894-95 series of "Five High Class Artists' Recitals" were also held on the palm-fringed stage of Ford Music Hall. The first was given on November 1 by the great piano virtuoso and composer Franz Xaver Scharwenka, whose "profound musicianship and deep insight" according to the *Pioneer Press* of November 2, 1894, delighted "an appreciative and cultured audience." The club cleared $120 on the concert. Scharwenka died suddenly about a month after his appearance in St. Paul. On December 6 the Rubinstein String Quartet, assisted by the twenty-one-year-old Brooklyn soprano Lillian Blauvelt, also appeared at Ford Music Hall, but the season's largest audience assembled at the People's Church at Pleasant and Chestnut streets on April 29 to hear the renowned Belgian violinist Eugene Ysäye.

This concert, which apparently cost the club $900, and the Scharwenka recital were unqualified financial successes and helped bring to fruition one of the club's early hopes — the encouragement of talented local music students through an educational loan fund established in the 1892-93 season. The fund benefitted further from recitals given on her second visit to St. Paul by the exceptional pianist Adele Aus der Ohe, by violinist Henry Marteau on his first American tour (tickets "$1.00 downstairs and .75 up") and by the lovable, erratic baritone Plunket Greene whose performance was said to have inspired "never ceasing, thunderous applause." Ella Richards, daughter of the exchange editor of the *Pioneer Press* and the first recipient of financial aid, was thereby assured study in Vienna under Theodor Leschetizky, one of the greatest piano teachers of all times. The loan fund idea was soon abandoned, however, because young musicians found it difficult to repay the sizable sums borrowed. Memorable, too, during these years was the recital in 1900 by Leopold Godowsky, a pianist so young, according to one critic, "that his years are all out of proportion to the prestige he has attained."

During the last years of the century the Schubert Club broke ground in yet another area by creating a student section — reportedly the first in the United States to be formed within a musical organization. Heretofore no one had paid much attention to the young musician, but during the presidency of Mrs. Dorr and her successor, Miss Shawe, talented youngsters were encouraged and provided with opportunities not only to perform in public but also to hear music and to practice and study it among their peers.

Two St. Paul girls, little Arma and Margaret Milch, were among the early student members of the Schubert Club. Arma was an eight-year-old violinist, and her sister, about eleven, played the piano. In 1898 they made their very successful debut before the Schubert Club. But so well developed was their technique that one newspaper reporter could not help wondering if they had "ever expended any moments in childish play." The Milch Sisters soon joined the Orpheum Circuit and went into vaudeville. Arma Milch Neff, now ninety-four, still lives in St. Paul. Today any qualified music student may become a member of the Schubert Club student section. When the student musician is considered ready for a public performance, he or she has the chance to play or sing in the club's student programs.

For a period toward the end of its first twenty years the club became involved in frequent activities with other groups. Musical programs sometimes took on the semblance of a cultural exchange. During the winter of 1894, for example, members chartered a private streetcar for a trip to Minneapolis to join in an afternoon of entertainment with the Thursday Musical group. A few years later the Minneapolis women returned the compliment by traveling to the capital city to honor Schubert Club members with a vocal and instrumental performance, and in 1909 the Matinee Musicale Club of Duluth gave an afternoon recital at Elks Hall facing Rice Park in St. Paul.

An experiment in co-sponsorship was less satisfactory. During the 1898-99 season the members joined with the Commercial Club of St. Paul to present a series of programs for the benefit of the public library building fund. The concerts were unqualified artistic successes, for they included such luminaries as the Metropolitan Opera Company's major Wagnerian soprano, Johanna Gadski, popular Welsh baritone David Ffrangcon-Davies, soprano Blanche Marchesi, and pianists Emil Sauer and Moriz Rosenthal. These recitals attracted capacity audiences, and about Miss Marchesi, for example, the *Pioneer Press* exulted: "In the whole musical history of the city no other artist has created equal enthusiasm." Another critic wrote of the same concert that the balcony of People's Church "harbored happily a stamping crowd." Unfortunately, the cost of the recitals so depleted the club's treasury that until the 1970s the group shunned similar co-sponsoring arrangements.

Concert planning had its difficulties then as now. Perhaps the most taxing job was —and still is — to guess which upcoming young artist might make the grade to stardom. Over the years the Schubert Club brilliantly enhanced its record of snaring gifted musicians of oncoming fame. Sometimes, however, it did guess wrong. In 1896 the French operatic soprano Emma Calvé, later to become one of the great singers of all time, was turned down as an unknown. Artists' fees continued high, too. When the officers considered American soprano Lillian Nordica, they thought her price of $600 too steep and engaged another performer. On May 4, 1898, on the other hand, the twenty-two-year-old pianist Josef Hofmann received $750, and Schubert Club members had to be urged by executive office Mrs. Charles E. Furness to "work hard for the success of this concert, that we may make it one of the great events in our Club history." And a spectacular success this Red Cross benefit was, even though the audience in the People's Church was not as large as the Schubert Club might have wished. According to the *Pioneer Press* critic, it was Hofmann's playing of the Franz Liszt arrangement of Wagner's *Tannhauser* overture, played upon request, that most electrified the listeners. "It brought . . . the audience to their feet with tense musical fervor, handkerchiefs were waved by fair hands [and] there were many cries of bravo." On the other hand a young California soprano of amazing vocal range, Ellen Beach Yaw, was fresh from her New York debut when she sang at Ford Music Hall in February, 1894. For her $100 fee she rendered only two solos and an encore.

By the mid-1890s concert hall rents had escalated, ranging from $50

to $100 for one evening. During the 1899-1900 season the requested rental
at People's Church for a series of five evening concerts and one matinee was
$575. As mentioned, artists' fees were even higher. For the 1895-96 season
$841 was spent for artists. At the same time, in the wake of a national finan-
cial depression in 1893, money was tight and ticket prices had to be kept low.
It is to the credit of the Schubert Club that entrance fees were held at "popular
prices" — seldom exceeding $1.50 —until the 1910 decade.

It was also a difficult struggle to enlist the support of some members
for the public concerts. Julia Dorr emphasized this in her president's report
for 1895, complaining that "Many of us have not yet waked up to the great
importance of hearing fine music at every possible opportunity if we would become broadly cultured." She urged members to coax their husbands, sons,
and brothers to attend the recitals. "Never mind if they grumble a little at first
at being dragged to concerts and lectures and pronounce them a bore," she concluded; the men would thereby "unconsciously become musically educated in
spite of themselves."

The woman who succeeded Mrs. Dorr as president, Elsie Shawe, was an
indefatiguable teacher, efficient organizer, and remarkably able supervisor, a
small yet imposing person who made up in energy what she lacked in physical
structure. She survived all her contemporaries, living from the early years of
the Schubert Club well into its new era as a public institution to become known
as "St. Paul's first lady of music." She died in 1962 at the age of ninety-six.

III. CONSOLIDATION AND "GOOD WORKS:"   1902-1930

By 1902 the Schubert Club's reputation was such that nationally known
musicians were eager to appear under its auspices. The club could virtually have
its choice of artists and was able to bring to the area the best music available.
Minnesotans were listening. Schubert Club members, therefore, devoted the
next three decades of their history to the consolidation of past efforts and so
broadening their membership and musical influence not only in St. Paul but also
throughout the region.

In 1902 a new president —Mrs. Warren S. Briggs — was elected to suc-
ceed Elsie Shawe. She was to serve for twenty-five of the next twenty-eight
years — the longest term of any elected officeholder — and, like Mrs. Dorr before her, displayed unusual administrative qualities and energies that soon made
her a force in the community. No better choice could probably have been made,
for it was her breadth of vision and real concentration on the job, combined
with a rich emotional responsiveness, which enabled her to develop at all times
a spirit of cooperation among the members. A meticulous administrator, a woman of domineering temperament and lofty vision, she more than other single

The People's Church, an acoustically
superior location for many Schubert
Club concerts from early in the century until 1940. Firemen with buck-
ets of water were at one time sta-
tioned in the balcony as a precaution,
The church burned down in 1940.

The young Jascha Heifetz who played
a recital for the Schubert Club in 1922
at the People's Church on Pleasant
Avenue .

The Kneisel Quartet

FRANZ KNEISEL, 1st Violin   LOUIS SVECENSKI, Viola
JULIUS ROENTGEN, 2nd Violin   WILLEM WILLEKE, Violoncello

PROGRAMME

Mozart   :   Quartet in B flat major.
Allegro vivace assai
Menuetto (Moderato)
Adagio
Allegro assai

a. Glière   :   Andante con variazioni from Quartet in A major, op. 2.

b. César Franck   :   Scherzo from Quartet in D major.

François Servais   :   Le Desir
Fantasie for Violoncello
WILLEM WILLEKE.

Schubert   :   Quartet in D minor, op. posthumous
Allegro
Andante con moto (Death and the Maiden)
Scherzo (Allegro molto)
Presto

PARK CONGREGATIONAL CHURCH

FRIDAY, JANUARY 28TH, 1910, AT 8:15 P. M.

STEINWAY PIANO USED

Mme. Mary Hallock, Pianist, of Philadelphia, will play in recital at the next regular meeting in Elks' Hall, Wednesday, February 23rd, at 3:45 P. M.

FLONZALEY QUARTET

(FOUNDED BY MR. E. J. DE COPPET, OF NEW YORK)
MANAGEMENT—LOUDON CHARLTON

ADOLFO BETTI, FIRST VIOLIN
ALFRED POCHON, SECOND VIOLIN
UGO ARA, VIOLA
IWAN D'ARCHAMBEAU, VIOLONCELLO

PROGRAMME

Beethoven . . Quartet in F major, op. 18, No. 1
Allegro con brio
Adagio affetuoso ed appassionata
Allegro Molto
Allegro

Jean Marie Leclair, Sonata for two violins, op. 12
(1687-1764)   Introduzione–Allegro con brio
(first time)   Largo–Giga
Gavotte–Allegro con fuoco

Mozart . . Andante cantabile

Dohnanyi . . "Scherzo" from the Quartet, op. 15

PARK CONGREGATIONAL CHURCH

WEDNESDAY EVENING, MARCH 8TH, 1911, AT 8:15

SCHUBERT CLUB presents
People's Church Auditorium
St. Paul, Minn.
Tickets exchanged at Field-Schlick Box-Office — Commencing
Thursday, November 5th -:- Annual Dues $5.00 and $3.00
FRIDAY EVENING
NOV. 6, 1936
at 8:15 o'clock
Lotte
LEHMANN
SOPRANO
Color plates by
permission of
"TIME"
Magazine
Edward Patston, Paul Hesse Studios Inc.

Elizabeth Dorsey and Mildred Ellerbe, faithful Schubert Club board members through the years. Miss Dorsey was particularly active in following recitals in New York and Europe and keeping a filing system of *New York Times* music reviews. Mrs. Ellerbe was President of the Schubert Club when the Keyboard Instrument Museum was begun.

Mrs. Stanley Hawks and Robert Moore who have attended many Schubert Club concerts down through the years. Mrs. Hawks is the daughter of Dr. W. W. Baldwin, the doctor and close friend of Henry James and several other celebrated expatriate artists living in Europe at the turn of the century.

Margaret Dean MacLaren who was a member of the Schubert Club for seventy years from 1911 until her death in 1981. Miss MacLaren is here photographed across the table while having lunch at the New French Cafe in Minneapolis with Schubert Club Executive Director Bruce Carlson in 1980.

Miss Ethelwyn Power, Schubert Club treasurer for over fifty years.

A seventeenth-century
Italian harpsichord in
the Schubert Club
Musical Instrument
Museum.

A photograph of the 1830 Kisting piano forte used by Brahms, Clara
Schumann, and other famous nineteenth century musicians. The first
instrument acquired for the Schubert Club Musical Instrument Museum.

A six and a half octave piano made by Conrad Graf in Vienna during the lifetime of Schubert and Beethoven, both of whom owned Graf pianos. This prized instrument in the Schubert Club Collection has recently been used for Schubert Club phonograph recordings by several prominent artists including Jorg Demus and Peter Serkin.

Schubert Club International Artists:
(Upper left and clockwise): Vladimir Horowitz, piano, 1928, 1979, and 1981 seasons; Olga Samaroff, pianist, 1924 season; Ossip Gabrilowitsch, pianist, 1903 season; and Myra Hess, pianist, 1925 and 1958 seasons.

person, except perhaps Julia Dorr, is identified with the Schubert Club during its first half century.

Of New England parentage, Florence Briggs graduated in piano, voice culture, and harmony from what was then the Potsdam, New York, State Normal School. In 1884 she came to St. Paul for her health and then studied and taught music until her marriage to Dr. Briggs, a prominent St. Paul physician. Mrs. Briggs joined the Schubert Club in 1892, the year of the first push for membership enrollment. And from then until her long tenure as president ended in 1930, she never spared her efforts to build the organization.

In her first presidential statement made early in 1903, Mrs. Briggs described in its *Yearbook* the club's development as it entered its twenty-first year. "The early days of infancy all the rapid growth of a life in its teens is outlived, and comes to its maturity in the full strength of a pride in its past and a healthful respect for itself as it stands, from which is born a natural faith in its future — a faith which is vital in that measure in which it is accompanied by good works."

The message might have sounded somewhat wordy, stilted, and forced, but it nonetheless was simple: The early years of the new century were indeed a time of "good works" for the Schubert Club. Elsie Shawe's philosophy of 1902 was also Mrs. Briggs': "We enrich ourselves by giving." Music, as the new president and her colleagues saw it, should not simply be a course of pleasure, though it was clearly and abundantly that. Music, they said, should uplift —-it had a moral and spiritual role to play, the same as churches and schools. The words "mission" and "moral," therefore, entered even more strongly into the club's vocabulary. In nearly everything the organization did, the didactic element reigned —teaching, helping, giving, and "good works."

During Mrs. Briggs' regime, the club in 1908 formed what it named an Altruistic Section to provide free musical entertainment for the enjoyment of the culturally deprived. Over the years members gave hundreds of programs at industrial plants and correctional facilities, orphan asylums, and other institutions. The program especially flourished under the dedicated supervision of Mrs. James C. Niemeyer who began direction of the work in 1928. This enduring phase of the club's activities caught the imagination of many St. Paul residents. When Mrs. Niemeyer retired in 1968 the programs continued with students performing for the elderly in rest homes. In 1976 the Schubert Club started a music therapy program for handicapped children and older people in homes and hospitals.

Another altruistic effort was a program for teaching underprivileged youngsters. It started in October, 1911, with a music class at the West Side Neighborhood House on Robertson Street under the direction of club member Mrs. Robert (Rose) Olds and Miss Clara M. Kellogg, head resident of the settlement. Worthy pupils, who wanted a musical education but were unable to pay for the training, received lessons at twenty-five cents per half hour under the watchful eyes of teachers from the ranks of the club's membership. The venture began with fourteen pupils. They eagerly took advantage of the opportunity to learn, and the class grew. Soon organizations like the International Institute and the Protestant Orphan Asylum asked for similar privileges, and before many years went by twelve such groups were being served

in St. Paul. Numerous pupils also competed for prizes of twenty-four free
lessons in piano, voice, or violin. At the end of each year a formal recital by
the most outstanding pupils from all the school branches was given at Dyer's
music hall.

By 1932 the Schubert Club Music School, as the group was called,
could boast a faculty of twenty-six teachers who gave two hundred lessons
a week in ten centers. It reached its period of greatest activity during the
depression of the 1930s. By 1958, however, the need for it was no longer
felt and this fundamental activity was brought to an end after forty-seven
years of unstinting service. Ten years later, in 1968, the community outreach
program called Project Cheer became a continuation of the old Neighborhood
House music school. Today it provides free after-school music training lessons
in the Summit-University area. The director, Mrs. Robert J. Harris, lives in
the district and with several teaching assistants provides lessons in piano, violin,
and guitar to over one hundred students a week. The popular program is ad-
ministered by the Schubert Club and financed largely by foundation grants.

It was also in 1912 that historian Henry A. Castle, in his *History of
St. Paul and Vicinity*, summed up the position of the then thirty-year-old Schubert Club when he wrote that "it has never held other than the highest standards; if St. Paul is, as all musicians from abroad declare, one of the most musical communities in the country, it is largely because this club has established
critical standards for itself, for the city, and has been discriminating at all
times."

The 1912-13 season witnessed six member recitals, six student concerts,
two of which were held in the evening, five studio teas, many study classes, and
three all-member meetings. During this busy time, busy for those days, that is,
the club also sponsored a series of "Young People's Popular Concerts" presented
by the St. Paul Symphony Orchestra. When the "admirable" Flonzaley Quartet
made its local appearance in November, 1912, as part of a concerted effort by
the club to present what were then called "novelties" and to popularize the music
of small ensembles, the *Pioneer Press* was lavish in its praise: "The musical public
of St. Paul," stated an enthusiastic reporter, "owes no small debt of gratitude to
the Schubert Club for its unremitting and highly successful efforts in behalf of
chamber music." While the Flonzaley attracted increasingly larger crowds to its
three successive yearly concerts before the Schubert Club, the Barrere Ensemble
in 1913 drew over 1,200 people —the largest audience ever recorded for a single
chamber concert in St. Paul to that date. In addition, one of the outstanding
early "novelties" took place in 1906 when Arnold Dolmetsch, a pioneer in the
reintroduction of early music literature on antique instruments, gave a recital
of "Music of the Olden Time" under the auspices of the club's student section.
The Dolmetsch program anticipated the Schubert Club's own present-day interest in early music, particularly as reflected in its museum of early keyboard instruments.

This same season also saw an attempt at self-analysis and a look into the
future. A symposium held in May, 1913, centered on a discussion of "The Schubert Club: Its Purpose, Scope, and Work." The topic was appropriate, for the
years ahead were to be difficult ones. One result of this conclave was the decision to admit men as special members, a proposition strongly plugged by both

names like violinists Jascha Heifetz and Jan Kubelik; contraltos Sophie Braslau, Julia Culp, and Louise Homer; pianists Rudolf Ganz, Percy Grainger, Ossip Gabrilowitsch, Myra Hess, and Ernest Schelling; baritone Reinald Werrenrath, bass Herbert Witherspoon, and tenor Tito Schipa, who are still remembered as great performers of their day. Soprano Hulda Lashanska's 1920 recital was "a genuine triumph," according to *Pioneer Press* critic James Gray who also noted that in 1921 pianist Benno Moiseiwitsch garnered "a well deserved ovation [from] an enthusiastic audience."

Mrs. Briggs, in her presidential greeting for 1923, pointed out that the club was "a St. Paul institution, rooted in the city's traditions, with its ear to the ground and alive to the day's work." Furthermore, she boasted, the organization's financial stability was excellent — a position gained "without underwriting or intensive campaign. Artists on our series," concluded the club's president, "although of superior merit, were artists not appealing to the speculative manager and, but for us, would not have been heard here in recital."

St. Paulites felt a vague sort of kinship with one of the period recitalists, contralto Louise Homer, since she had once spent almost three years of her girlhood as a minister's daughter in St. Paul and Minneapolis. When she returned to St. Paul and the Schubert Club in 1913 to present a second concert before what was called a "splendid audience. . . flowers galore and a demonstration at the close of the concert," her listeners especially appreciated the tribute she paid local composer Leopold Bruenner when she sang his song setting of Edgar Allen Poe's *Eldorado*. The price tag for this second visit, however, was $1,000.

The St. Paul appearance of Heifetz on January 26, 1922, typifies the continuing perspicacity of sharp-eyed club officers in choosing young and little-known performers of superlative talent. Violinist Heifetz was a "miraculous boy" who had not yet reached his majority when, on his first American tour, he electrified a capacity audience (including critic Flandrau) with the "sentimental loveliness" of Max Bruch's *Concerto in G Minor*. (A similar "scoop" thirty-nine years later was the appearance of soprano Leontyne Price.) Two other promising young unknowns presented during the early 1920s were pianist Moiseiwitsch and violinist Toscha Seidel. At about this time a so-called "matinee series" became a sort of proving ground for upcoming young artists. Pianists Vladimir Horowitz and Nikolai Orloff, who performed in the afternoon, were among those later engaged for evening concerts. These trial programs ended with the depression years.

The sponsoring of artists over a long span of time is certain to result in occasional criticism of the choice of recitalist as well as a few less than satisfactory performances. To the Schubert Club's enduring credit, its percentage of disappointments has been low. In November, 1924, reviewer Ned B. Abbott of the *St. Paul Daily News* was critical of a group of songs in English that tenor Richard Crooks presented, calling them "sop." But the most abysmal failure in all the hundred years of Schubert Club history (at least in the eyes of several qualified local newspaper critics) was the recital presented by the Metropolitan Opera star Mario Chamlee and his wife, soprano Ruth Miller, on December 2, 1926. Abbott's review of the concert in the *News* the following day was devastating — a refreshing change from the bland notices in the two local newspapers after the departure of Flandrau and before the advent of James Gray and Frances Boardman as critics on the *Pioneer Press* and *Dispatch*.

"Whether Mr. Mario Chamlee, tenor, doesn't know any better," complained Abbott, "or whether he considers St. Paul the 'sticks' and thinks we don't know any better, somebody ought to tell him that according to the Schubert Club's artistic standards his recital last night . . . was perilously near a joke . . . . Programing such songs as 'Goin' Home,' 'Liebestraum,' 'Dawn,' 'Moon Marketing,' 'The Old Refrain,' etc., are hardly calculated to engender serious consideration of him as an artist.

"The 'St. Sulpice Scene' from *Manon* done in costume, while not successful from an artistic point of view . . . served to demonstrate that the operatic stage and not the concert platform is where both Mr. Chamlee and Miss Miller belong. One felt that here the singers were at home despite the strain on the imagination watching Manon steal through the cloistered confines of St. Sulpice via the port side of a grand piano." Frances Boardman, critic on the *Pioneer Press*, echoed her colleague, adding that "The recitalist must *know* . . . how to make a concert program. This is something that operatic artists frequently do not know anything about."

Abbott, however, hastened to absolve an undoubtedly embarrassed impresario: "One has no disposition to criticize the Schubert Club for this concert," he concluded. "It was merely a case of guessing wrong, a matter easily forgiven when one remembers [soprano Maria] Kurenko and [pianist Alfred] Cortot."

On the other hand few concerts ever matched the all-out sensation made by pianist Vladimir Horowitz. Early in March, 1928, two months after his New York debut, he performed at an afternoon concert in St. Paul. Critic Abbott astutely observed that, although "not yet a full-fledged artist . . . he will not only be heard, but heard of often as the years go by." Horowitz's October, 1928, return engagement for an evening performance, however, produced what another *Daily News* reporter, William H. Marzolf, called a "well-behaved riot" among the usually undemonstrative members of the Schubert Club. According to Minneapolis critic John K. Sherman, this event was "probably the most exciting 'one-man show' . . . by any musical artist in the twenties."

The overflow audience outdid itself in showing enthusiasm and delight. Frances Boardman left the most memorable vignette of a triumphant Horowitz, his formal program ended, playing encore after encore. "So loathe were the listeners to part from the slender young wizard," she reported, "that they refused to leave the spot even after two stalwarts appeared for the obvious purpose of removing the piano from the stage with the result that the stalwarts retired, and Mr. Horowitz obliged once more." Miss Boardman, nevertheless, did qualify her laudatory review in the *Pioneer Press* of October 31 by noting that Horowitz was too preoccupied with his own virtuosity and "put himself too much between the audience and the composer." Marzolf made essentially the same comment in more forceful phrases, calling the pianist a technician, but not yet an artist. Both were convinced that this tendency would disappear with the increasing maturity of the young performer. Beyond any doubt,

Mrs. Briggs and Leopold Bruenner, director of the St. Paul Choral Art Society. There were stipulations, however. The men had to be passed on by an executive committee of club ladies, and they would not be allowed to vote. It is interesting to note that while men around the country were considering the fitness of allowing women the franchise, the women of the Schubert Club were deliberating at some length on club suffrage for their male members.

During the summer of 1913 the club launched another membership drive. The new rules enabled any musically interested person to join the Schubert Club at the reasonable rate of $3.00 a year for actives, students, and "special" (meaning the men) and $5.00 for associates (that is, subscribing listeners). Consequently the directors opened all its public artists' concerts free to members and ordered that — except to non-residents of St. Paul — no single admission tickets would be sold. All non-Schubert Club members were thereby barred from recitals after the close of the ticket sale campaign, a regulation that would hold for nearly thirty years.

In 1914 memberships reached a peak of 1,232, making it the second largest music club in the United States. But from that point on membership steadily dropped until, by 1916 and the beginning of World War I, it was down to 811. To make matters worse, the disasterous April, 1915 fire at the St. Paul Public Library, located at the corner of St. Peter and Seventh streets, destroyed all the club's study material, sheet music, and many of its manuscript records and scrapbooks going back to 1882. The club reached another low point in 1918 when only 574 St. Paulites could be counted as dues-paying supporters, and it was found necessary to move the evening concerts from the People's Church (where it had been held for two years) back to the smaller Park Congregational Church (later called Plymouth Congregational) located at Holly and Mackubin streets. A local businessman in 1916 deplored the lack of musical interest among the capital city's 275,000 residents. Aside from Schubert Club events, he complained, "St. Paul . . . has had but one public artists' recital during the season and that by John MacCormack. . . . And the worst of it is," he concluded sadly, "that we seem perfectly satisfied to have it so."

The organization did not accept these discouraging setbacks without a struggle. On September 13, 1915, it optimistically incorporated under the laws of Minnesota. In an effort to overcome the wartime indifference to cultural activities, the energetic Mrs. Briggs traveled widely and gave talks, arguing that the Schubert Club's work was needed more than ever as an educational force and as an agency to lighten heavy hearts during war years. She pointed out that "Volumes of testimony from Government officials, from Army and Navy, in camp, field and on the sea, and from great masses of civilians urge music as essential, a war-time need." The public was apparently unconvinced, however, for not until 1919 did the club's membership once more exceed a thousand.

By 1919 and the end of the war the public concerts were once again back at the People's Church with its spacious hall and ideal acoustics. For several decades this was to remain the Schubert Club's home. Although Charles M. Flandrau, a popular local critic and author, apparently thought the building garishly decorated and vulgarly lighted, it was possibly one of the best auditoriums that St. Paul has ever had, and throughout most of the 1920s and 1930s it was the city's musical center. The St. Paul Municipal Auditorium

Theater saw its first Schubert Club concert in 1919 when Metropolitan Opera soprano Mabel Garrison gave a performance for the American Friends of Music in France. The Auditorium did not come into regular use by the club, however, until the 1940s.

Minnesota's oldest and largest musical organization entered its vigorous fifth decade with a constructive program and a burgeoning enrollment of over 1,300 members. During the 1920s there were all of twenty-four committees covering almost every musical project imaginable; in 1904 there had been seven. One of the features of its fortieth anniversary celebration was an appeal for volunteer subscriptions to strengthen the newly formed scholarship fund devoted to the encouragement and perpetuation of competitive trials for gifted young musicians. This program replaced the unsuccessful scholarship loan fund of the 1890s. At first the fund was slow to grow, so as a stopgap measure three one-year scholarships had to be hastily raised by special subscription so they could be awarded during the 1922-23 season. The first of many scholarship auditions to come was held early in February, 1923. They marked the beginnings of what today is one of the Schubert Club's major spheres of action: giving young people a chance to compete for prestige scholarships and thereby encouraging them to continue their musical careers. Several other funds have since been established, such as the Mrs. R. E. Van Kirk Discretionary Prize (1927), the Maud Taylor Hill Scholarship and Marion Ramsey Furness Scholarships (both in 1957). These and frequent annual memorial gifts today make a major contribution to the musical education of many Midwestern students. In all, over $100,000 has been paid out since 1923 in competitive and discretionary scholarships to deserving aspirants from Minnesota and neighboring states.

The major activity of the Schubert Club, and its most expensive, has over the years continued to be the public artists' series. In the early 1900s, after the financial difficulties of the decade before, the concerts were characterized by greater novelty and more scrupulous attention to the pocketbook. Though always solvent, the club had taken some rough bumps and was bent on pursuing another road. Mrs. Briggs summed up the monetary position in 1903. In a statement quoted at length in the local press, she warned the St. Paul public that it would hear only as many concerts as it was willing to pay for. "The Schubert Club," she concluded, "gives to its members to the limit of the amount of its membership, and to the public to the limit of its patronage. More than this good judgment forbids." Such tactics paid off, and so successful were these appeals that the club membership rose dramatically to a peak of over 1,600 in 1926. In 1921, for example, Mrs. Briggs reported that "an enrollment of nearly fourteen hundred members has necessitated the engaging of People's Church for seven instead of the usual three concerts." This schedule of seven concerts a season was more or less continued until 1930 when the Great Depression set in and the Schubert Club's enrollment once again declined.

Those pre-crash days were golden years for concertgoers in St. Paul. The Schubert Club's progressive program during the Briggs' administration continued to be reflected in the artists it made available to the citizens of the Twin Cities area. There was glamour, luster, and box-office appeal in

Horowitz's Midwestern debut was an outstanding, triumphant success, and those who heard it can still vividly recall how the very foundations of the People's Church seemed to shake during his madcap crescendos and fortissimi.

Throughout the period the club's public concerts continued to be impressive, and more often than not they represented first appearances either in the Twin Cities or the Northwest. On two occasions in the mid-1930s the club sponsored American debuts — those of German soprano Ria Ginster in 1935 and American pianist Anne Mundy, a St. Paulite, in 1936.

IV. "VENTURESOME CONSERVATISM:" 1930 - 1958

At the close of the 1929-30 concert season, Mrs. Briggs' long tenure as president ended. Under her strong leadership there had been a slow but noticeable change in the club's basic structure. Despite sporadic opposition to her program, Mrs. Briggs had been democratizing the organization. She swept away many membership restrictions and most vestiges of the small, socially exclusive group it once had been. She especially emphasized that the club should never become a mere "managerial agency who . . . conducts his business for . . . profit." In her final report to Schubert Club members she stressed the intangible results of her many years as president — the awakening of an appreciation for music, the development of musical abilities in the young, and the increased emphasis on the annual series of artists' concerts. "There is nothing to see," she summarized, "no temple made with hands, no imposing monument . . . nor have we aimed at such." When Mrs. Briggs died in September, 1941, Frances Boardman emphasized the long fight of this "devoted and far-seeing woman" on behalf of chamber music.

Another name holds a special place in the story of the Schubert Club's first half century. Mrs. Frank L. Hoffman was for many years after 1900 an active member of the organization. Although never a featured artist on any of its musical programs, she frequently made herself available to the club as an accomplished piano accompanist. Born in Joliet, Illinois, Mrs. Hoffman, then Katherine Collins, became the organist at the Cathedral of St. Paul in 1897. A chance request brought her international recognition. When the great operatic contralto Ernestine Schumann-Heink gave a recital at the People's Church in 1906, Mrs. Hoffman was invited to assist at the concert. So impressed was the singer that immediately after the performance she asked Mrs. Hoffman to become her permanent accompanist. In that capacity the St. Paul pianist traveled widely over the globe, performed before kings and emperors, and studied musical interpretation in Vienna under composer Richard Strauss and conductor Felix Weingartner.

1882
1949
Robert & Gaby Casadesus
ST. PAUL AUDITORIUM THEATRE
FRIDAY, FEB. 18, 1949
8:30 P.M.

1882
1948
65th Anniversary Concert
HELEN TRAUBEL
Dramatic Soprano, Metropolitan Opera Association
ST. PAUL AUDITORIUM THEATRE
MONDAY, APRIL 5, 1948

The Saint Paul Auditorium Theater, site of Schubert Club International Artist Series concerts from 1940 to 1968.

The demolition of the St. Paul Auditorium Theater in 1983; the site was being cleared for the new Ordway Music Theater.

Brenda Ueland, writer and occasional music critic for the *Minneapolis Times.* The post-World War II years in the Twin Cities, when Ueland was reviewing, sparkled with contemporary music led by Dmitri Mitropoulos, Louis Krasner, Ernst Krenek, Tom Nee and others.

AN EXCERPT FROM A BRENDA UELAND REVIEW

(From a review in the Minneapolis Times, *December 2, 1943;
note the reference to Schubert Club member Marjorie Briggs.)*

There was a dazzling concert at Hamline College, in that red stone castle with the spindly tower. The concert room is so charming and small and it curves all around the tiny stage. And so does a delicate wooden balcony. The audience can almost reach down and pat the musicians gratefully.

It was free. And seven pre-eminent musicians took part, five of them world famous: Mitropoulos, Ernst Krenek, Joanna and Nikolai Graudan and Victor Babin.

Say that Grieg were exiled and Nina Greig, Schumann, Joachim, Cesar Franck, etc. --- that driven out of Europe they found an obscure livelihood here, nobody knowing much about it, and say they began to blow on the spark of living music to keep it alive --- Well that is how it is.

First Ernst Krenek (he teaches at Hamline) described the music we were about to hear. It was "modern" music. They would expound it for us. It is that music we rage against (when we pay to hear it), throwing ourselves around in our seats like a horse in a shell-hole. As for Mr. Krenek (solid, steady, blue-eyed, the son of a Czech officer in the old Austrian army), his operas were performed all over Europe. Then he foreswore the old way of composing for "modern" music. They have played his music at the Symphony and I didn't like it (my fault, my limitation) and jeered for a while until I discovered that people who really know something — Mitropolous, the Graudans — say that it is excellent, important.

First Mrs. Briggs played piano pieces by Roger Sessions (a leading American composer who teaches at Princeton). And I thought they were beautiful, though I had to keep my mind pried open in a humble, effortful way. You see in listening to new music there is a frustration. It is because your mind can not pour along it freely as when you hear Beethoven's Fifth Symphony or the Swanee River. You are checked, blocked. The tune never goes where you think it will. Fatigue comes then and you give up trying. And probably go home saying: "Terrible! Like streetcars screeching as they go around a curve." But it isn't so.

Then Mme. Duschak (slim, black-browed, utterly charming) sang Charles Ives' songs and Mitropoulos, (wearing round glasses on his handsome Dantesque nose) played the piano for her. The songs were certainly queer. But I wouldn't allow my Philistine self to flounce off indignantly. I pinned all my understanding on each note . . . .

International Artist Series poster of the 1942-1943 season. Isaac Stern returned to Saint Paul in 1983 and appeared on the International Artist Series celebrating the 40th anniversary of his first appearance in St. Paul.

Mrs. Webb Raudenbush,
Schubert Club President,
1933-1943.

Schubert Club Luncheon and Board Meeting at the Minnesota Club in 1937.

(Right)
Mrs. Frank Lightner;
Mrs. Louis Hill, and
Mrs. William Dorsey,
faithful Schubert
Club board members
through the years,
here photographed
during the Schubert
Club's 75th Anniver-
sary Year, 1957.

(Below)
Mrs. John G. Ordway
and Miss Anna
Furness, Schubert
Club board members
at a post-concert
reception in 1944.

FIRKUSNY
Celebrated
Czech Pianist

SCHUBERT CLUB
SEASON 1944-45
Bidu Sayao, Soprano; Adolf Busch and
His Little Symphony, with Eugene
Istomin, Pianist; General Platoff Don
Cossack Chorus; Todd Duncan, Bari-
tone; Rudolf Firkusny, Pianist.
Season Tickets (5 Events):
$5.00, $4.00, $3.00, $1.50 (plus 20% tax)
On sale at: Field, Schlick Box Office

Irmgard Seefried

ST. PAUL
AUDITORIUM THEATRE

Thursday, April 17, 1958
8:30 p. m.

The great English contralto Kathleen Ferrier was a favorite musician of Bruno Walter,
Sir John Barbirolli, Benjamin Britten, her accompanist, Gerald Moore, and many others.
Her premature death at the age of forty-one put a tragic end to one of the greatest
singing careers of our time. Kathleen Ferrier sang at a Schubert Club recital at the St.
Paul Auditorium in 1949 just four years before her death. This photograph is by Cecil
Beaton.

Schubert Club International Artists:
(Upper left and clockwise): Elizabeth Schwarzkopf, soprano, 1954 season; Dietrich Fischer-Dieskau, baritone, 1955 season; Emanuel Feuermann, cellist, 1935 season; and Artur Rubenstein, pianist, 1942 season.

Nor was the "indomitable Ernestine" Katherine Hoffman's only musical associate. The pianist's unusual abilities won her repeated engagements with Fritz Kreisler, Herbert Witherspoon, Johanna Gadski, Edward Johnson, and other ranking artists. In St. Paul, Mrs. Hoffman assisted to critical acclaim at the Schubert Club evening recitals of contralto Merle Alcock in 1921 and soprano Lucrezia Bori in 1922. Near the close of her colorful career, she not only summarized her personal experiences but by inference spoke out in behalf of musical organizations like the Schubert Club which were responsible for the wide dissemination of good music. "It is impossible," she told a *Pioneer Press* reporter, "to acquire a musical education without constantly hearing performances of every sort."

During the palmy pre-depression days the yearly program was once again extended, this time to seven major afternoon and evening concerts. By 1930, however, these had to be reduced to five evening recitals — a number adhered to until 1961, when for a decade it was cut down to four. Since the 1971-72 season five concerts a year have again been presented. The largest sum paid for performers in the 1920s was close to $5,000 for the 1926-27 season. Today the price tag is over $50,000 for a total of five recitals. Yearly rentals of the People's Church auditorium varied from $300 to $450. At the St. Paul Auditorium the cost for the 1968-69 season, for example, came to $1,000. Today the Schubert Club has to pay some $8,000 per season as rental fee for five concerts at the O'Shaughnessy Auditorium, College of St. Catherine.

Early in the 1930s new leaders of the Schubert Club brought about occasional policy changes, but these internal alterations were of little interest to the public. Efforts to liberalize the membership rules, however, were of general concern, and they were continued under the presidencies of Mrs. Charles A. Guyer and Mrs. Webb R. Raudenbush (the latter for ten years from 1933 to 1943). They also brought a new, less aggressive tone to the office of president.

One outstanding development of the 1930s was the club's increased support of American music and local composers. In time this expanded to include Minnesota composers. As early as April, 1901, for example, the Schubert Club organized a program at Mozart Hall which included only the music of American composers. A 1925 recital offered a Schubert Club ensemble performing a *Quintet for Piano and Strings* by Donald Ferguson, distinguished professor of music at the University of Minnesota. A 1926 performance of American music featured the works of four individuals "distinctively associated with Minnesota musical resources" — Arthur Bergh, Arthur Koener, Frank Bibb, and George Klass.

Club interest in the local creative artist assumed a more organized form in 1936 with the creation of a "Manuscript Study" section under the chair of a local composer, Mrs. Paul Bremer. Opened to all members who were "engaged in the composition of music or its study," the group met monthly to hear talks and discuss their works. Each season generally was capped with a radio broadcast of local music. Through this group, as reported in a Twin City newspaper, "a great wealth of talent came to light and a widespread interest in the art of writing music was revealed." On April 1, 1940, a historic concert of all-Minnesota music was presented at the Hamline University Norton Field House. The program, sponsored by the Schubert Club, was the first formal concert ever devoted exclusively to the works of Minnesota composers. The club's interest in original works written by local musicians did not end with the discontinuance of the Manuscript Study section in the spring of 1945. The Schubert Club continued to be what John H. Harvey in 1952 called "conservatively daring." They joined the College of St. Catherine to organize a Minnesota Composers Forum during the 1950s and went on to sponsor several programs of modern Minnesota music. Through the 1970s to the present the Minnesota Composers Forum has continued to be closely allied with the Schubert Club which has taken as its most recent endeavor the commissioning of works by area composers.

The year 1940 found the Schubert Club at a crossroads. Charter member Marion Ramsey Furness died in 1935, and with her perished the last remaining link with the pre-Schubert Club past — the days of Borup, Oakes, and neighborly at-home gatherings around the melodeon. In 1938 came the death of Louise Dorr at the age of eighty-five, a woman whose impact had been so tremendous that the club minutes perhaps erroneously described her as "the organizer" of the Schubert Club. And then again, perhaps not.

Florence M. Raudenbush, Weimar-educated, in 1933 became the tenth woman to head the group with her cultured German musical background. She capably led its twenty-three committees for a decade — the second longest tenure in the club's history. It was a temporary war-related move to Illinois in 1943 that forced her resignation. The years of depression were among the most difficult faced by the organization since the days of World War I. The determined efforts of an able Mrs. Raudenbush and her board, however, prevented the great loss in membership which had been experienced in those earlier war years. Five concerts a season remained the rule, and the sharp-eyed ability of the club's officers in obtaining talented artists never slackened. There was no decrease of interest in the scholarship plan, in the music lessons for underprivileged children, nor in the work with young people and professionals. Membership fees remained at the modest figure of $5.00 a year, with $3.00 for students.

Yet there were occasional problems. In 1934 Frances Boardman of the *Pioneer Press* wrote an article criticizing the "sartorial formalities" of the evening recitals. In this worst depression of American history the conspicuous wealth of a formidable battery of elegantly and expensively gowned officers of the Schubert Club, carrying an air of privilege and power, underscored the yawning discrepencies between the "haves" and "have nots" and grated on the the public nerve. "I can see both sides of the questions," Miss Boardman wrote — "to do pleasant honor to a distinguished recital . . . However . . . a good many people . . . are uncomfortably overwhelmed sometimes to the point of staying away." It was not too many years, though, before these "dress circle" formalities faded and casual clothing became the order of the day. The barriers between public frustration and private exclusivity were being cast aside, and the Schubert Club was becoming increasingly democratic.

Near the end of her successful ten years in office, Florence Raudenbush faced one of the most drastic readjustments in the history of the Schubert Club. In 1939 the People's Church was closed and then sold to become the Catholic Community Center. Concerts for the 1939-40 season continued in its audito-

rium, the fourth recital being presented late in February by the talented and
decorative contralto Elizabeth Wysor. During the early hours of March 22,
1940, however, fire swept with explosive rapidity through the tinder-dry wooden
interior of the firetrap building.. By the time twenty pieces of fire equipment
answered the alarm, the holocaust was out of control, and the Schubert Club
was confronted by an unexpected emergency. With the season's fifth and final
concert only two and a half weeks away, the officers had to move fast. They
engaged the theater section of the St. Paul Auditorium, and the return engagement of tenor Richard Crooks after an absence of fourteen years took place as
scheduled.

The vast St. Paul Municipal Auditorium Theater, with its 2,651 seats,
was certainly not the best of recital halls for the Schubert Club. The auditorium's management was basically cooperative, but sometimes unpredictable.
So-called firm dates were changed if more lucrative bookings came along. The
building itself was unattractive and inhospitable with cold, drafty balconies,
shabby and garishly painted hallways, uncomfortable facilities for the performers, and general tackiness. The appearance of the stage setting, at least, was
considerably improved when new antique gold velvet curtains were first used
at the January, 1949, concert presented by the English pianist Clifford Curzon
during his first United States tour. John Harvey thought they "made the stage
look like the setting for a concert instead of, as in the past, a setting for a play
called *Murder In A Warehouse.*" Yet, for lack of anything better the Auditorium
Theater remained home for the Schubert Club for thirty years, the locale of many
magnificent musical moments.

For the next two seasons after 1940 the Schubert Club followed its
long-established rule of confining audiences to the yearly subscription list, but
since the Auditorium Theater was twice the size of People's Church and the annual rental considerably higher, this plan soon proved financially unworkable.
During 1942-43 the main floor was still reserved for holders of membership
cards, but the two balconies were thrown open to the general sale of single tickets.
This semi-restrictive policy lasted only one year; in 1943-44, under the presidency
of Mrs. Julian E. Gilman, the entire auditorium became available to the public,
and the word "membership" was dropped from all publicity. The Schubert
Club had at last gone public.

In 1943 the Schubert Club presented its first Black soloist, the attractive
soprano Anne Brown of the original *Porgy and Bess* Broadway production, who,
in the words of critic Boardman, was a "singing artist of such superlative gifts
and craftsmanship as seldom adorn any concert season more than once, if at all."
Miss Brown's sponsors encountered prejudice, however, when they tried to secure
lodgings for her in the city's hotels. Complaints, it is said, were also heard because
a fourteen-year-old Black music student and her mother used membership tickets
given them by a local music teacher and actually sat downstairs in "aisle seats,
second row, center section." Officers of the Schubert Club did what they could
to counteract these attitudes by engaging for the next season the popular Black
baritone Todd Duncan.

The club has since presented a number of the finest Black singers available
within its price range, including sopranos Ellabelle Davis in 1953, Mattiwilda
Dobbs in 1955, Shirley Verrett in 1964, and in 1976 the electrifying and commanding

soprano Jessye Norman. But not many concerts in the Schubert Club's long history have equaled the sensational 1961 Twin Cities debut of Metropolitan Opera soprano Leontyne Price who only shortly before had made an impressive debut at La Scala in Milan, Italy. For perhaps the first time, area newspapers reported, the "Standing Room Only" sign hung outside the theater section's box office. The "stunning" Price concert ended, according to John H. Harvey of the *Pioneer Press*, "in a blaze of vocal glory," making more than one long-time concertgoer recall with pleasure the excitement of Vladimir Horowitz's October, 1928 concert at the People's Church.

Near the end of the Schubert Club's seventh decade one unusual event took place which created no small stir in the local press. The Paganini Quartet's St. Paul recital on January 20, 1948, will be long remembered, not so much because of the good chamber music heard that evening, as for a mysterious, dark-haired stranger and his bold, successful masquerade. When the quartet's four musicians reached the auditorium early that evening, a middle-aged, bespectacled gentleman dressed in evening clothes met them at the entrance. He obviously knew his way around the theater and immediately took charge of things onstage, seeing that the chairs and music stands were placed correctly and instructing the electricians how best to direct the spotlights. He escorted the performers to their dressing room and then retreated unnoticed. Officers of the Schubert Club thought him the quartet's business manager; the artists took him for an official of the club. At the end of the concert four violin bows, valued at about $1,200 were missing. When last seen, shortly after the concert began, the thief was boarding a Minneapolis-bound streetcar. Removing the four bows from under his coat, he carefully placed them across his lap and rode west into oblivion. Following the Paganini incident the Auditorium Theater's backstage security was tightened, and for future protection the Schubert Club immediately took out liability insurance.

The club first departed from its usual policy of presenting only individual musical artists and small ensembles when it brought to St. Paul the Carmelita Maracci Dance Group in November, 1941. Since then three similar companies have packed the auditorium with enthusiastic audiences: The Roberto Iglesias Ballet Español in 1959 (the Schubert Club's first ballet), José Limon and Dance Company in 1961, and the Alvin Ailey American Dance Theater in 1969. Other memorable concerts during these later years up to 1958 included those of Isaac Stern (1943, 1947, and 1951); pianist Maryla Jonas (1947); a repeat recital by the great English pianist Dame Myra Hess for the seventy-fifth anniversary series in 1958; singers Kathleen Ferrier (1949) and Irmgard Seefried (1952 and 1958); and pianist Clifford Curzon who at the close of the first selection on his program (either in 1949 or 1955) stood up, glanced questioningly into the depths of the piano, and slowly reached down to remove a tuning fork from its innards.

By the mid-1940s the Schubert Club found it difficult to make ends meet. Expenses increased, and there was growing competition from other concert courses in the Twin Cities. To cover one year's deficit the club had to borrow money for the first time, a necessity which made board members realize in 1947 that a guarantors' fund was perhaps the only solution to their growing money problems. Soon, however, the group needed more than just a guarantee of support. In 1949, therefore, an annual subscription appeal was instituted and money was given outright. Yearly fund drives continued thereafter until 1954 when under the presidency of Mrs. Seigel A. Anderson, the Schubert Club became a part of the newly formed St. Paul Council of Arts and Science and made the transition from a private club to a non-profit civic organization. No longer was the Schubert Club a club.

Such, then, were the first seventy-six years of the Schubert Club when it still had some vestiges left, although very few, of an exclusive organization, a self-contained female entity aimed at doing "good works" and bringing musical education to the people of St. Paul. Theirs was the classic role of the musical club, according to critic John K. Sherman, "organized by energetic women who viewed civic uplift in terms of musical improvement." It was a peculiarly American institution, and the women had done it on their own, with little or no help from the opposite sex. They had every right to be proud of the club's illustrious history. That for three-quarters of a century the women had the care and spending of large amounts of money, without once overspending, was, according to columnist Amy Birdsall, something of a miracle. There were those who thought that the Schubert Club was probably the only organization of women in the country that could boast such a high accomplishment. The club's greatest contribution overall since 1893 has been the presentation to St. Paul of some of the world's greatest musicians. No one has better summed up the problems the women ran into over the years than John Harvey. There were several ways to solve them, he told readers of the *Pioneer Press* on April 22, 1951. "One way is to play safe and present artists known by performance to be sure-fire boxoffice draws. Another is to gamble with a group of unknowns. A third is to mix sure things with calculated risks. It is to the credit of the Schubert Club that, operating with a modest budget and on a narrow margin of security, it traditionally has followed the third policy of venturesome conservatism." Such a course will not always fill theater seats with enthusiastic audiences; sometimes it brings criticism. In the long run, however, the policy demonstrates the organization's continuing vitality.

So with 1958, on its seventy-sixth birthday, came the end of an era for the Schubert Club, St. Paul's matriarch of music. Over the years it had moved away from its image as a "ladies group" to become an integral part of the St. Paul cultural scene.

❧◎❧

Elly Ameling, soprano, outside the Commodore Hotel
during her appearance at the Schubert Club Summer
Vocal Festival in the summer of 1975.

Gerard Souzay, baritone, has appeared on several Schubert Club recitals,
master classes, and with Elly Ameling in the 1975 Summer Vocal Festival.
Here photographed at the art deco Wurlitzer piano in the Schubert Club
Keyboard Instrument Museum.

Alicia de Larrocha appeared on the Schubert Club International Artist Series in 1969, 1973, 1977 and during the Centennial Season, 1983.

Isaac Stern appeared on the Schubert Club International Artist Series in 1943, 1947, 1951 and during the Centennial Season, 1983.

A concert under water in the Schubert Club Contemporary Music Program. Hoses with whistles on one end were connected to the showers; by varying the water pressure different underwater pitches and sounds were achieved. Co-sponsored in 1973 with Walker Art Center.

Max Neuhaus explaining his sound installation project at the Como Conservatory. Co-sponsored in 1978 with Walker Art Center.

(Left)
Composer John Cage at the 1868 Chickering piano in the Schubert Club Keyboard Instrument Museum. Turning pages is Roy Close, Music Critic of the St. Paul *Dispatch* and *Pioneer Press.*

(Below)
Mezzo-soprano Frederica Von Stade back stage at O'Shaughnessy Auditorium after a Schubert Club recital in 1979. At right is Schubert Club board member Nancy Shepard.

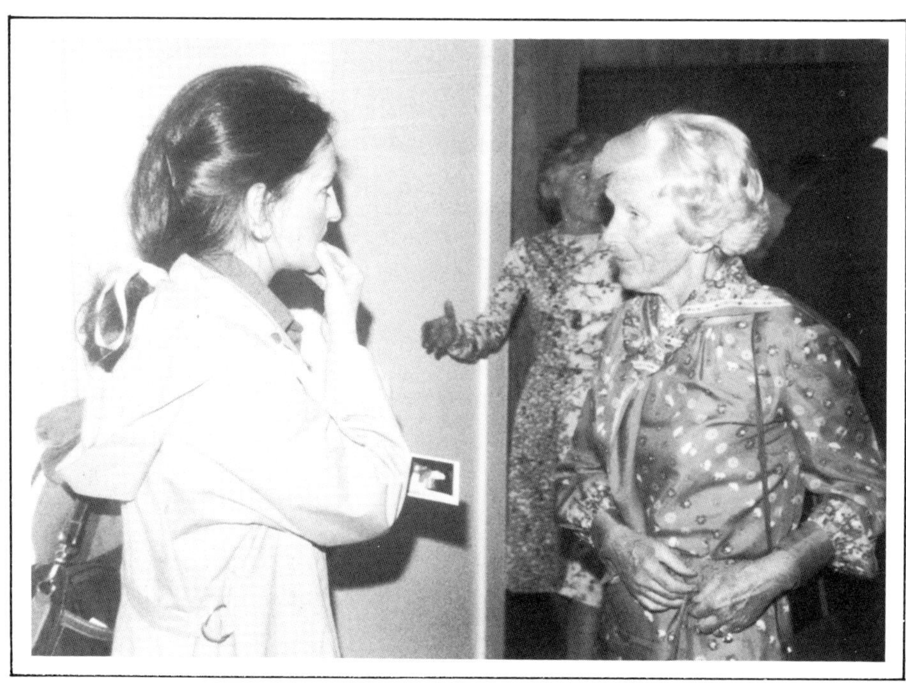

Mary Griggs Burke, Marvin Pertzik and Pat Hart, friends and board members of the Schubert Club photographed in the Schubert Club Keyboard Instrument Museum.

I. A. O'Shaughnessy Auditorium at the College of Saint Catherine, the location of the Schubert Club International Artist Series concerts from 1970 to 1984.

St. Paul Pioneer Press, October 18, 1976

Soprano Jessye Norman displays superb control

By JOHN H. HARVEY
Pioneer Press
Music Critic

If one were to say that Jessye Norman has not quite yet arrived, it is not because of lack of present accomplishment but because of seemingly limitless potential.

The 31-year-old American soprano, who made her local debut under Schubert Club auspices, has sung a wide variety of operatic roles from Handel and Mozart to Verdi, Berlioz and Wagner as well as works in other forms by numerous composers, both here and abroad.

She has a voice of substance and darkly glowing burnish already suitable to big dramatic roles.

CRITICS CORNER

Judging against her recordings several years back, she seems to have ironed out whatever technical problems she had.

Saturday night's program had no operatic showpieces; it was devoted rather to German lieder and French art songs. And in these she showed superb control of dynamic gradations and evenness of vocal quality which enabled her to spin out a pianissimo with perfect tonal consistency.

Miss Norman's major work was Schumann's cycle "Frauenliebe und Leben." Today one has to make certain adjustments to the Chamisso text. From a modern point of view the young woman's self-abasement and fulsome adoration of her godlike man can make even a confirmed male chauvinist squirm.

Miss Norman, however, put herself right into the mood and attitude of sentimental German romanticism which evokes Schumann's exquisitely beautiful musical response. She sang the songs as though she believed every syllable. It was a sensitive, expressive performance which carried the listener with it.

Schumann's "Talismane," with its wide range and forceful expression, served as a warm-up piece for Miss Norman's big voice before she settled into the intimacies of "Die Lotusblume," "Widmung" and the song-cycle.

A prominent feature of all of these was the singer's flexible, seamless handling of the vocal line. This carried over into the French songs as well.

Among the singers with whom Miss Norman has studied are Pierre Bernac and Gerard Souzay, and she was keenly aware of the styles, moods and atmospheres of the songs of both Poulenc and Duparc and communicated them beautifully.

They included the former's "Voyage Paris," "Monteparnasse," "La Grenouilliere" and "Les Chemins de l'Amour" (where she transfigured the cafe-chantant style while retaining its flavor), and the latter's "Chanson Triste," "L'Extase" and "L'Invitation au Voyage."

She concluded with a group of spirituals. For the beauty and emotional impact of these, one has to go back to Marian Anderson for a parallel.

Her accompanist was Dalton Baldwin, whose sterling artistic partnership throughout the evening was, of course, no surprise.

John Harvey, Music Critic for the St. Paul *Pioneer Press* and *Dispatch* from 1945 to 1980, photographed with his daughter Eleonora.

Handbills publicizing some of the chamber ensembles
which have appeared under Schubert Club auspices.

Earl Carlyss, violinist from the Juilliard String Quartet, at the Minneapolis-St. Paul International Airport with Nigel Redden, former Director of the Performing Arts at the Walker Art Center, Minneapolis.

Anne Voglewede and Sharon Carlson from the Schubert Club staff, and Linda Twiss (center) from the Saint Paul Chamber Orchestra, selling tickets before a chamber music concert at Janet Wallace Fine Arts Center. This series is co-sponsored with the SPCO and Walker Art Center.

Landmark Center,
Saint Paul, Minne-
sota, home of the
Schubert Club of-
fices and Keyboard
Instrument Museum.

Pinchas Zukerman and Neville Marriner appearing as guests with Minnesota Public Radio
host Larry Richardson on the live radio broadcast series "Live From Landmark". This
series is broadcast on Thursdays at noon from the Frederick King Weyerhaeuser Auditorium and is co-sponsored by the Schubert Club and Minnesota Public Radio.

John Steinway viewing an early American grand piano (a Gilbert piano with a Steinway label stencilled on it) in the Schubert Club Keyboard Instrument Museum.

Martha VonBlon, Schubert Club Administrative Assistant for seven years, on a luncheon break in the cortile restaurant at Landmark Center.

(Above)
Jean-Pierre Rampal giving a master class for the Schubert Club at Macalester College, Janet Wallace Recital Hall.

(Right)
Samuel Sanders, pianist for many Schubert Club visiting artists (including Mstislav Rostropovich, Beverly Sills and Itzhak Perlman). Mr. Sanders gave a master class on accompanying for the Schubert Club in June of 1983.

The staff of the Minnesota Composers Forum, who have occupied space in the Schubert Club offices since 1976. Jodie Williams, Administrative Assistant, Lila Jacob, Managing Director, and Managing Composers, Libby Larsen, Randall Davidson, and Stephen Paulus.

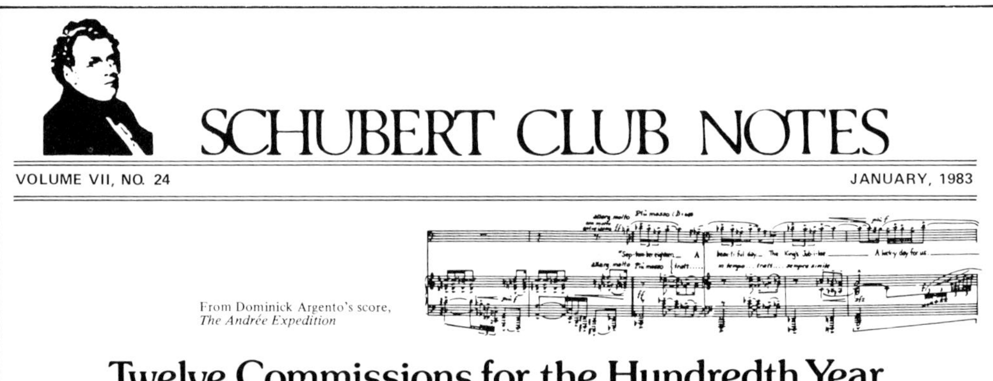

"The Schubert Club Notes" is published quarterly and sent as a newsletter to International Artist Series subscribers as well as other interested individuals. The winter issue of 1983 announced twelve pieces of music commissioned by the Schubert Club during its 100th year, including those by John MacKay, Jr., Dominick Argento, Libby Larsen, Joan Tower, Stephen Paulus, Paul Schoenfield, Janika Vandervelde, Randall Davidson, Stanislaw Skrowaczewski, and Paul Fetler.

Schubert Club Music Therapy Sessions:
(Top) Music therapist Ann Marie Huck (standing) at Bridgeview School, St. Paul.
(Above) Adelaide Gordon and Peg Woellner with music therapist Pat Ilika at Courage Center, Golden Valley, Minnesota.

THE SCHUBERT CLUB PRESENTS

Masterpieces of the British Film

HENRY V with Lawrence Olivier and *October 31, Nov. 1.*
Renee Asherson (1944)

november 7, 8.　　THE HORSE'S MOUTH starring
Alec Guiness (1960)

THE CRUEL SEA with Jack Hawkins, *november 14, 15.*
Richard Attenborough

november 28, 29.　　TALES of HOFFMANN with the
Royal Ballet - Moira
Shearer, Principal (1951)

FREDERICK K. WEYERHAEUSER AUDITORIUM, LANDMARK CENTER, 75 W. FIFTH ST., ST. PAUL

ALL FILMS START AT 8:00 P.M.　　ADULTS: $1.75　　CHILDREN UNDER 15: $1.00

Posters announcing various series of films sponsored
by the Schubert Club in downtown St. Paul, Friday
and Saturday evenings.

SHAKESPEARE
ON FILM

RICHARD III
OCTOBER 3 & 4, (col.) Directed by Laurence Olivier, Starring
Laurence Olivier and John Gielgud

AS YOU LIKE IT
OCTOBER 10 & 11, (b/w) Directed by Paul Czinner,
Starring Laurence Olivier and Elizabeth Bergner

HAMLET
OCTOBER 17 & 18, (col.) Directed by Tony Richardson,
Starring Nichol Williamson and Marianne Faithfull

JULIUS CAESAR
OCTOBER 24 & 25, (col.) Directed by Jason Robards,
Starring Charlton Heston and Jason Robards

A MIDSUMMER NIGHT'S DREAM
OCTOBER 31 & NOVEMBER 1, (col.) Directed by Peter Hall,
Starring Diana Rigg and Bill Travers

OTHELLO
NOVEMBER 7 & 8, (col.) Directed by Stuart Burge,
Starring Laurence Olivier and Maggie Smith

MACBETH
NOVEMBER 14 & 15, (col.) Directed by Roman Polanski,
Starring Jon Finch and Francesca Annis

THE TAMING OF THE SHREW
NOVEMBER 21 & 22, (col.) Directed by Franco Zeffirelli,
Starring Elizabeth Taylor and Richard Burton

TICKETS AVAILABLE AT THE DOOR — $1.75 GENERAL ADMISSION
$1.00 MEMBERS OF SPONSORING ORGANIZATIONS

ALL FILMS WILL BE SHOWN AT 8:00 P.M. in the St. Paul Arts & Science
Center Auditorium, 10th and Cedar, St. Paul.

Sponsored by The Schubert Club and the Minneapolis Society of Fine Arts

Harold Feder, President of the Fisher Nut Company and St. Paul arts enthusiast, on the cover of the International Artist Series brochure.

The Schubert Club International Artist Series 1983-84 Season: **Yo-Yo Ma,** Cello, October 2; **Leontyne Price,** Soprano, October 9; **Ken Noda,** Piano, November 11; **Claudio Arrau,** Piano, March 3; and **Pinchas Zukerman,** Violin, May 13.

V. A NEW ERA BEGINS: 1958 - 1983

During the middle years of the twentieth century, following the end
of World War II, St. Paul was in the doldrums. Urban residents were moving
to the suburbs; the downtown area, deteriorating, was becoming unattractive
and tacky (much like the Auditorium Theater); and suburban malls were
drawing the shoppers. St. Paul, so young when Mark Twain visited in 1882,
was indeed showing his age. The situation had become so serious that drastic
changes were imperative. Sparked by the 1949 passage of federal urban re-
newal legislation, an in-depth survey was ordered, and during the spring of
1951 the results were released. Among other problems besetting St. Paul
besides deteriorating city neighborhoods and a dying downtown, the report
showed that culturally the city was on what it called a starvation diet. Nor
did the future look particularly bright. Obviously something should be done
to draw together those organizations interested in music, theater, arts and
crafts, the dance, and leisure-time activities. Not enough support was available for them all, and for the most part there was a lack of cooperation among
the several agencies.

One suggested solution was a community arts center, a central headquarters which could serve as a clearing house, obtain monetary help from
the city and its citizens, and thereby bring St. Paul back to its earlier cultural
leadership. "Each organization," the report concluded, "must stand or fall
on the money it can get to keep it going." The Schubert Club was a prompt
and enthusiastic supporter of the idea for intercultural harmony and in 1954
immediately joined the newly formed Arts and Science Council as a charter
member. By 1957 the Council had made such progress in its planning that
Mrs. Charles E. Porter, the club's first delegate to the Council and a former
president, could report that "From a loosely knit and sometimes unsteady
group, it has become a surprisingly solid and cohesive organization with great
hopes for the future." Beginning in 1959, annual appeals for money were
made through cooperative and coordinated United Arts Fund drives which
continue today, and in June, 1963 ground was broken for a new three-million-
dollar arts and science center at 10th and Wabasha streets. In January, 1965,
the city's major cultural institutions moved from two old houses, a run-down
church, and a succession of private homes and rented offices into a handsome
new building occupying a full city block on the edge of the downtown area.
For the Schubert Club, this long-anticipated event marked another important
milestone. At the advanced age of eighty-two the organization at last had
what it thought would be adequate rehearsal, meeting, and office space in
its first permanent home. No longer was the president's home the club's office where files and all records were kept. No longer did their business have
to be transacted in living rooms or around dining tables. The moveable offices of earlier days were no more.

Many advantages followed, and the alliance helped stimulate cooperative efforts and strengthen the Schubert Club's growing reputation as a
public institution. There came, as well, a wider sense of communication

with other cultural organizations and with the community. The blessings of the new quarters, however, proved short-lived. Only a little more than five years later, space was already tight at the Center. But help was in sight. During the 1960s the handsome 1902 Federal Courts Building on Rice Park was threatened with demolition by an area business seeking more office space. Fortunately such a catastrophe was avoided through the dedicated help of a few far-sighted St. Paul citizens. Soon this impressive structure was to provide the ultimate solution for the space problems of, among others, the St. Paul Schubert Club.

The 1960s were development years for the Schubert Club, too. For lack of a better recital hall, concerts still had to be held in the vast, drafty, dingy Auditorium Theater. But changes here were also in the offing. During July, 1968, under the presidency of Mrs. Kenneth O. Johnson, the club made another important decision — to hire a man and place him as the club's salaried manager, the first male, with the exception of the Schubert Club choral and orchestra conductor Emil Oberhoffer, to break into the solid ranks of this exclusively female and volunteer organization. That was when Bruce Carlson came over from Minneapolis to become today's Executive Director. Under his dedicated direction the club has been able to move ahead dramatically.

The 1960s also produced a musician who could well be called the Schubert Club's outstanding protege and scholarship winner. Daniel Chorzempa, organist and pianist of Polish-Alsacian ancestry, was born and grew up in Minneapolis and by the age of seventeen had garnered a total of five Schubert Club scholarships. In mid-January, 1964, when only nineteen, he made his first formal appearance before the club, to the delight of local critics. Three years later, on April 14, 1967, Chorzempa was featured on a "Showcase" daytime concert which critic Harvey in the *Pioneer Press* called "one of the most exciting events of the season" — that in face of an established pianist who had performed that season, Rosalyn Tureck. Chorzempa's third recital in St. Paul was on a Sunday in May, 1971. It was "a most impressive display of solid musicianship and sensitive interpretation," Harvey noted, calling him "a musician of uncommon stature." The club also sponsored an organ recital by Chorzempa in Minneapolis a week later. Daniel Chorzempa called the Schubert Club "my faithful supporters," and of all the club's officers through the years no single person was more dedicated to or interested in the futures of young and talented musicians (including Chorzempa) than the late Elizabeth Dorsey, an unassuming, shy, quiet, capable woman who since 1921 had devoted so much time and generous personal help in the service of the Schubert Club and the arts in St. Paul. Today Chorzempa continues his work in Germany as both organist and pianist, concertizing, cutting recordings of Bach, Handel and Saint-Saëns' organ music for prestigious companies like the Dutch firm of Philips, composing electronic music, and building a solid European reputation. From the press in England and on the Continent have come remarkable plaudits for this musician's "prodigious talent," thus justifying the faith of the Schubert Club and of Elizabeth Dorsey.

Other active Schubert Club members can also be counted among these scholarship and grant winners who have gained recognition in the music field: a 1924 winner, Howard Laramy, became a leading baritone with the

American Opera Company; mezzo-soprano Ann Bomar and pianist Anne Mundy, both of St. Paul, also stand out nationally. So do pianist Mary Briggs and soprano Sara Jane Fleming who sang with the New York City Center Opera. St. Paulite Joan Logue, soprano and talented performer of both classic and avant-garde music, who has gained considerable recognition in Italy, is especially interested in electronic technology. Most recently guitarist Sharon Isbin of Minneapolis has made a mark among scholarship winners, as have violinist Kathleen Winkler of Minneapolis and cellist Tanya Remenikova. The New York debuts of the last three have been sponsored by the Schubert Club, and early 1983 also saw two more club-sponsored debuts in New York, those of Timothy Paradise, clarinet, and Lynn Aspnes, harp. These scholarship awards and special grants, a part of the regional music scene since 1923, remain today one of the most important contributions of the Schubert Club to the growth of music in the Upper Midwest. Funding for these endeavors often comes from the Jerome Foundation program for emerging artists set up by Jerome Hill, son of Maud Taylor Hill who, for many years was active in the Schubert Club.

The 1960s were also years of experimenting — trying out new ideas and dropping them if not successful enough to pay their way. A contemporary music seminar was tried, as were the daytime "Showcase" and a "Debut" series, among others. The club also experimented with concerts broadcast over radio station KSJN. These later developed into the successful weekly noontime broadcasts of carefully chosen Minnesota and visiting musicians, "Live From Landmark," which are today aired every Thursday during the fall, winter, and spring months. These once again bring the music of local musicians into the home, as was common before the turn of the century.

Cooperative efforts with other cultural organizations were tried again during the 1960s. One of the more successful was in 1966 when the Schubert Club, the St. Paul Civic Opera, and the St. Paul Philharmonic Society conducted by Leopold Sipe, joined to give four well-received performances of a full-length opera, *The Ballad of Baby Doe,* with music by Douglas Moore, which was a "sparkling success" according to the St. Paul *Dispatch*. It was also called a good example of what joint efforts of groups in the city could produce cooperatively, and was one of the many proofs to come that the Arts and Science Council was helping to produce outstanding results.

Of the evening artists' concerts presented by the Schubert Club during the 1960 decade, several stand out over others. For example, the aftermath of the Mstislav Rostropovich cello recital on November 4, 1963, must have brought consternation to the club's officers. It seems that the artist's New York manager was irritated when he later talked to the club's concert committee. First, he claimed the attendance was nothing to boast of. Unfortunately the concert took place in the oversize Auditorium Theater only six days after that of pianist Robert Casadesus, one of the club's most popular artists. In addition, according to the taped reminiscences of Mrs. Samuel Hunter, the manager thought the performance was given only a lukewarm review by what he said was a free-lance writer. And, finally, he criticized St. Paul for provincialism and blamed the Schubert Club for poor promotion and not "keeping the critic in line." The reviewer who covered that concert for the *Pioneer Press* was the thoroughly professional, capable, long-time critic John H. Harvey whose job in the newspaper was to review with intelligence well over a hundred performances a year. In 1963 Harvey had been performing that service for eighteen years — hardly what one would call a free-lance writer. His review of that Rostropovich recital, when read today, seems to be a very fair appraisal. For instance, he called the artist's technique "fabulous," his fingering "amazingly clean." This was the only known time that the ladies of the Schubert Club had to deal with an irate manager and with managerial complaints. There is no record of what the cellist had to say, since he was forbidden to speak English. Rostropovich, however, soon defected to the United States and returned to St. Paul in November, 1981, to perform again before a warmly receptive Schubert Club audience.

Then there was the sensational Shirley Verrett recital on the last day of November, 1964, of which John K. Sherman stated in the *Minneapolis Star* that the "enterprising Schubert Club has again scored a scoop." At the end of the mezzo-soprano's stunning performance there was a standing ovation, the first since the Leontyne Price concert. But those were the days when such signs of enthusiastic approval by the Schubert Club really meant something. During March, 1966, contralto Maureen Forrester returned after an absence of seven years to give the Schubert Club what Harvey termed "one of the great vocal events hereabouts in a number of seasons." Finally, Korean violinist Young Uck Kim, age eighteen, presented a stunning concert of "superior quality" on March 18, 1968. Again the local newspaper lauded the Schubert Club for its "almost perennial success in picking high class artists in the bud."

Minneapolis critic Peter Altman summed up this decade of the 1960s in the *Star*: "Perhaps the most unusual feature of the local cultural scene," he wrote in the issue for November 28, 1968, "is the variety and high standards of the local groups [like the] Schubert Club." He added that "groups like St. Paul Opera, Minneapolis Institute of Arts, and the University Artists Course suffer from excessive conservatism. They need to be jarred from complacency." The Schubert Club and the adventurous Walker Art Center of Minneapolis were just the ones to do that in the 1970s. In the meantime the St. Paul club did what it could. Two offbeat concerts of the late 1960s anticipated what could well be in store for the future. The first, in August, 1967, presented the "comfortably schizophrenic world" of comic Peter Schiekele and his musical slapstick P.D.Q. Bach program. This was a new field for the club, and one Minneapolis critic claimed that St. Paul was charmed. Then in April, 1969, pianist Peter Serkin, son of Rudolf, also gave a different type of recital — one featuring pulsing lights "that didn't quite mesh." The 1970s were to bring more special and extra concerts, some of which perhaps would not be to everyone's liking, but which certainly would make people sit up and take notice. The first of a number of such efforts was a rock musical, *The House of Leather*, presented at the Crawford Livingston Theater in the summer of 1969 and witnessed mostly by young people.

If a definition were needed for the role of the Schubert Club in the 1970s, it might be found in the statement of new executive director Carlson —

Peter Serkin at the Graf piano from the Schubert Club Keyboard Instrument Museum. In May of 1983, Peter Serkin began a series of recording projects for the Schubert Club and Pro Arte Records which includes works by Schubert as well as the last six Beethoven sonatas.

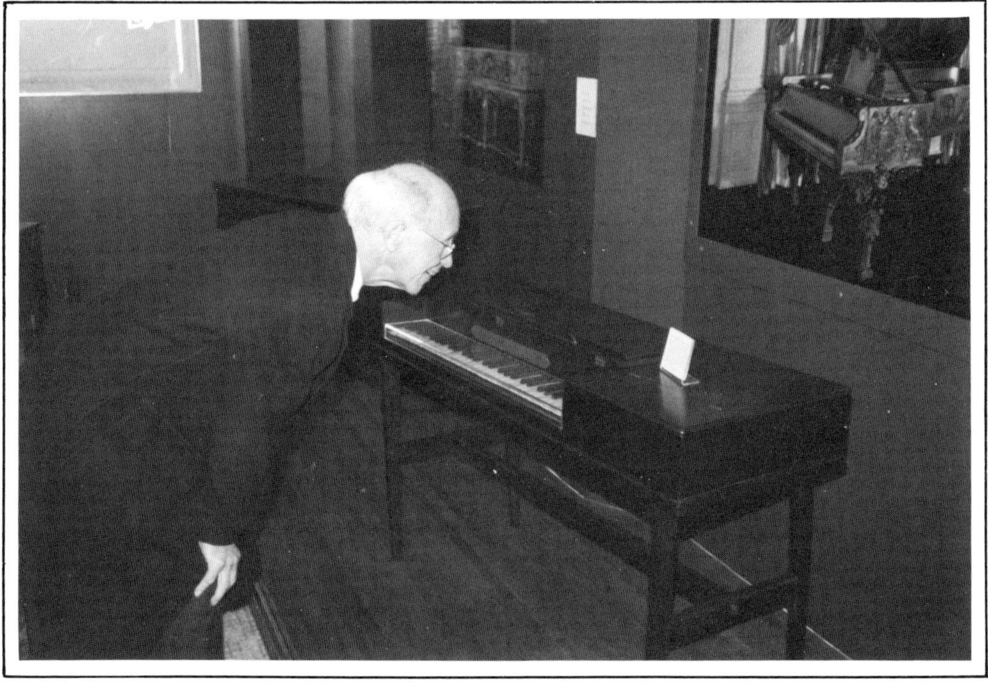

Rudolf Serkin peering at the 1768 Zumpe piano in the Schubert Club Keyboard Instrument Museum. This Zumpe piano is particularly important to the Schubert Club as the recital tradition was begun on a Zumpe piano in a concert by J. C. Bach in London in 1768.

Andrew Wolf (Isaac Stern's pianist) and (left to right) John Musser and Richard Dietrich, at a reception following Isaac Stern's Schubert Club recital in 1983. At the back, right table, Betty Musser, John Myers, Isaac Stern, and Rosalyn Pflaum.

Mstislav Rostropovich, cellist, with his daughter, pianist, Elena Rostropovich, and Tanya Remenikova (center) at the reception after a Schubert Club recital in 1981. In the back, Lois Cooper and Gustav Johnson, chairman of the Schubert Club International Artist Series.

Dominick Argento was commissioned by the Schubert Club in 1974 to write a song cycle *From the Diary of Virginia Woolf* which was premiered by the English mezzo-soprano Janet Baker, January 5, 1975 at Orchestra Hall in Minneapolis. This magnificent work was later performed by Dame Janet Baker at Carnegie Hall in New York City and won the Pulitzer Prize for Music in 1975.

Dominick Argento receiving a silk embroidered emblem of a balloon at a Centennial Dinner at the American Swedish Institute. Commissioned by the Schubert Club to write a song cycle in its Centennial Year, Argento chose his text from the journals of the voyage of Swedish aeronaut S. A. Andrée. Schubert Club Executive Director Bruce Carlson is at left.

Schubert Club board member, Jeanne Shepard, to whom *The Andrée Expedition* was dedicated, and baritone Håkan Hagegård at a post-concert reception following the premiere performance of this Argento song cycle.

THE SCHUBERT CLUB
KEYBOARD INSTRUMENT COLLECTION

❡

DEDICATION
in honor of

CHARLOTTE ORDWAY & POLLY WALLACE

❡

4:30 P.M., November 30, 1981

Music:	Anne Voglewede, Signe Ilstrup, Yuka Suzuki (Schubert Club staff)
Remarks:	Mr. Bruce Carlson Executive Director
Plaque:	Mrs. Thomas F. Ellerbe, Jr. Chairman, Museum Committee
Gift:	Mrs. Donald Sell President
Songs:	Mrs. William Jenkins, soprano Mrs. Donald MacGregor, piano

Program of the ceremony which dedicated the Schubert Club Keyboard Instrument Museum to Charlotte P. Ordway and her Schubert Club Friends, and honored the generous support of Polly Ordway Wallace.

Schubert Club board members Jeanne Shepard and Jane Matteson with Polly Wallace (center) in the Schubert Club Keyboard Instrument Museum.

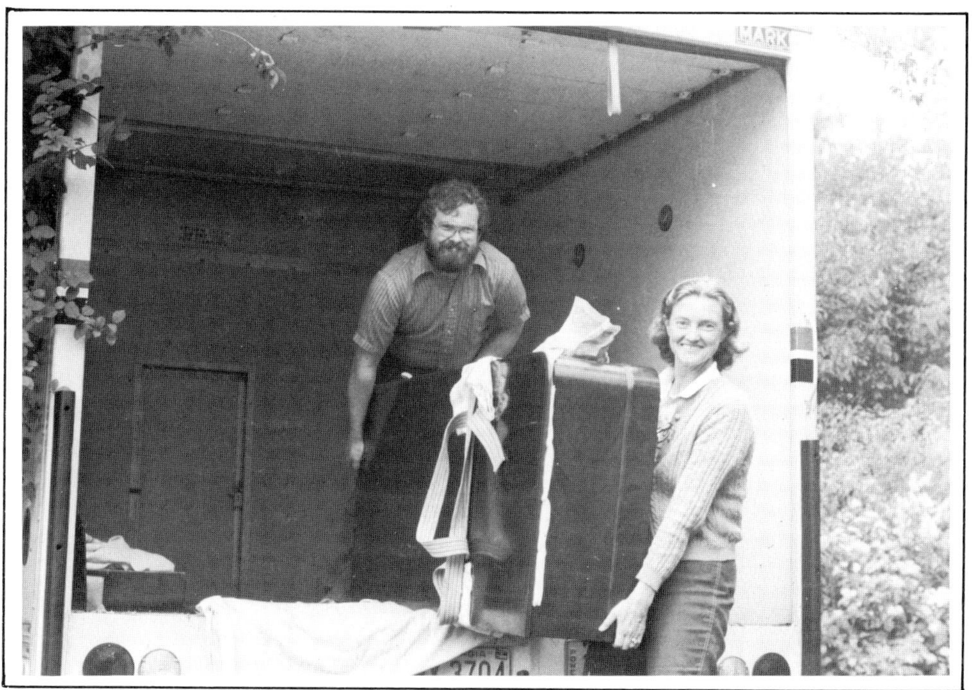

Richard Sorensen, Schubert Club conservator, and Charlotte Drake, Schubert Club
board member, loading a Geib and Walker square piano, a gift to the Schubert
Club Keyboard Instrument Museum from the family of Foster Hannaford.

George Reid, a member of the Schubert Club Keyboard Instrument
Museum committee, speaking with Thelma Hunter, Schubert Club
board member, at a Museum opening. At right, Robert Matteson,
Nancy Weyerhaeuser, and Jeanne Shepard.

Ann Slosser, Chairman of the
Scholarship Committee and
Pat Hart, Chairman of the
Student Section. At right,
Estelle Sell, Schubert Club
President.

Jane McKim and Diana Barsness, active board members
of the Schubert Club, working on the Student Section
auditions.

(Left)
Daniel Chorzempa, inter-
nationally celebrated or-
ganist and keyboard artist
(and winner of five Schu-
bert Club scholarships)
at the 1868 Streicher
piano in the Schubert
Club Keyboard Instrument
Collection. At left, Bruce
Carlson, Schubert Club
Executive Director.

(Below)
Carol Wincenc, flutist,
and Sharon Isbin, guitar-
ist, with composer Joan
Tower (center). Ms.
Tower was commissioned
by the Schubert Club in
its Centennial Year to
write a piece for flute
and guitar which was
premiered by Ms. Isbin
and Ms. Wincenc in
April, 1983.

Cover of the Schubert Club booklet published on the occasion of the Keyboard Instrument Museum's first exhibition, "The Piano: Mirror of American Life" which opened on February 22, 1981. The booklet is a collection of five essays which trace the development of the piano and its significance in American history.

1840 Erard piano used and signed by Franz Liszt, now owned by The Schubert Club Keyboard Instrument Museum and featured in the exhibit "Composers and Their Pianos."

Je déclare avoir fait force fausses notes et gribouillé maint mauvaise musique sur ce charmant instrument

19 Juillet 44 F. Liszt

French inscription underneath the lid of the 1840 Erard piano signed by Liszt. Translation: "I confess having made false notes and scribbled bad music on this charming instrument."

On November 2, 1982 the exhibition "Composers and Their Pianos" opened in the Schubert Club Keyboard Instrument Museum. Instruments used by famous composers were featured. Malcolm Bilson played a recital on historical Schubert Club instruments as part of the exhibition's opening.

Jorg Demus appeared on a Schubert Club International Artist Series concert at O'Shaughnessy Auditorium in 1982 using several early pianos. He also made a one and one–half hour radio broadcast on National Public Radio using instruments from the Schubert Club Collection. Photographed here with Helen Hollis, the wonderful consultant to the Schubert Club Keyboard Instrument Museum from the Smithsonian Institution.

Jorg Demus, Viennese pianist who performed on the Schubert Club International Artist Series in 1982, having breakfast at Moudry's Apothecary Shop at St. Peter and Fifth streets in downtown St. Paul.

Michael Barone, Music Director of Minnesota Public Radio, and Bruce Carlson, Schubert Club Executive Director, planning the "Baroque and Beyond" series, co-sponsored by Minnesota Public Radio and the Schubert Club in 1983.

(Above)
Richard Sorensen, Schubert Club conservator, in the Schubert Club Keyboard Instrument Museum working on a reproduction of a 1784 Stein pianoforte, an instrument commissioned by the Schubert Club during its centennial year.

(Right)
William Kugler, proprietor of the Kugler Musical Instrument Museum in St. Paul. The Kugler Museum has been an inspiration to the Schubert Club; plans for cooperative ventures have been discussed for fifteen years.

A view of the construction of the Ordway Music Theater in June, 1983.

Harold Schonberg, of the *New York Times*, viewing a model of the Ordway Music Theater and discussing this new concert hall with project director Henry Blodgett.

Larry Williams, Landmark Building Superintendent, hanging a Schubert Club banner in Rice Park. Members of the Schubert Club 100th Anniversary Committee: Meredith Alden, Ruth Huss, Thelma Hunter and Estelle Sell, with Barry Cohen and David Blackman, grouped below.

Schubert Club Presidents:
(Front row): Mrs. John Neimeyer, Mrs. Seigel Anderson, Mrs. John McNeill, Mrs. Gordon Shepard, Mrs. Charles Porter; *(Back row):* Mrs. S. Axel von Bergen, Mrs. Leonard Olson, Mrs. Kenneth O. Johnson, and Mrs. Henry Kartarik.
Photograph taken in 1975 at the home of Mrs. John McNeill, 1979 Summit Avenue.

(Above)
Estelle Sell, President of the Schubert Club during its Centennial Year, with former Schubert Club presidents, Harriet Abbott and Marge Porter at the Centennial Dinner at hotel St. Paul.

(Left)
Harold Schonberg, senior music critic of the New York *Times* (1960-1980), guest speaker at the Schubert Club Centennial Dinner, with Mary Ann Feldman, Schubert Club International Artist Series committee member and program editor of the Minnesota Orchestra.

Harold Schonberg *(New York Times)* and (left to right) Irma Vallecillo, Paul Sperry
with Stephen Paulus and Michael Dennis Browne. Mr. Paulus was commissioned
by the Schubert Club to write a song cycle based on poems about the visual arts.
Mr. Browne was commissioned to write one of the poems.

Nancy Latimer, George Latimer (St. Paul Mayor) with composer Stephen Paulus at the
hotel St. Paul Centennial Dinner, May 11, 1983, where Paulus's *Artsongs* was premiered.

Estelle Sell, Schubert Club President, 1979-1983, with incoming President-elect Karyn Diehl at the Schubert Club Annual Meeting in June, 1983.

Thelma Hunter (left) and Julie Himmelstrup (right), Schubert Club board members, with tenor Paul Sperry and pianist Irma Vallecillo at the Schubert Club Centennial Dinner in May, 1983.

Patricia Hampl, author of the prize-winning book *A Romantic Education*, (Houghton-Mifflin) and of several Schubert Club commissions, with Brenda Ueland, author of *If You Want to Write* and the autobiography *Me*, both re-published by the Schubert Club in 1983).

Miss Elizabeth Dorsey, Schubert Club board member for over fifty years, and Alicia de Larrocha, guest artist on the International Artist Series en route to a luncheon at the Lexington Restaurant.

Schubert Club International Artists:
(Upper left and clockwise): Dame Janet Baker, mezzo-soprano, 1975, 1982 seasons; Lynn Harrell, cellist, 1977 season; Rudolf Serkin, piano, 1961, 1977 and 1980 seasons; and Vladimir Ashkenazy, pianist, 1961, 1974 seasons. Photographs autographed by the artists for the Schubert Club archives.

Schubert Club International Artists:
(Upper left and clockwise): Jessye Norman, soprano, 1976 season; Beverly Sills, soprano, 1970, 1972, 1975 and 1979 seasons; Marilyn Horne, mezzo-soprano, 1974, 1980 seasons; and Frederica Von Stade, mezzo-soprano, 1979 season.

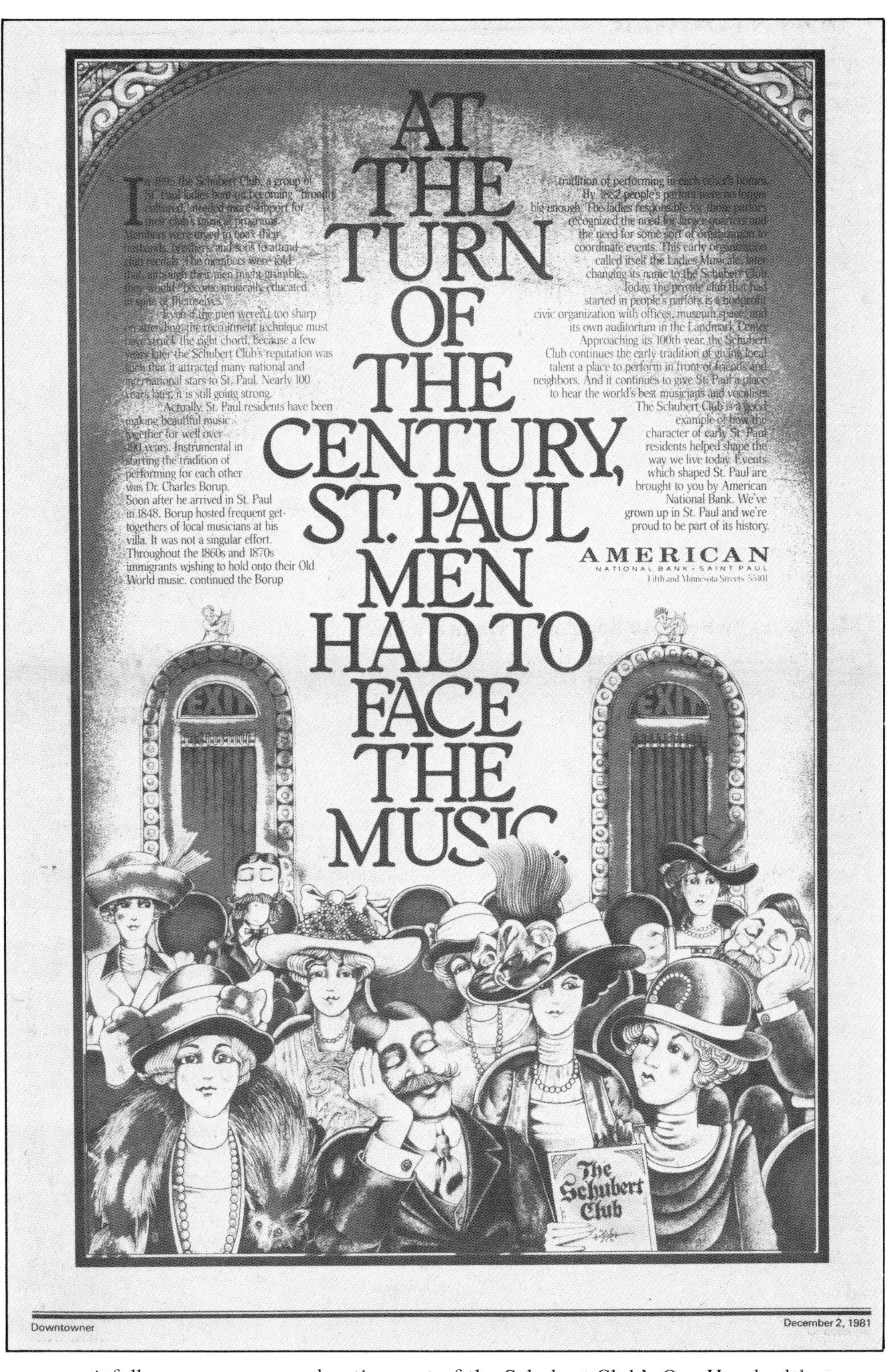

A full-page newspaper advertisement of the Schubert Club's One Hundredth Anniversary sponsored by the American National Bank of Saint Paul.

that "with the Schubert Club you are not tied down to a certain formula.
If there is something that has interest and musical value, you can put it on."
Provided, of course, it wouldn't lose too much money. And that is exactly
what the club did with such flair during the last decade of its hundred year
history. The old lady began kicking up her heels!

The club entered the 70s with an all-time high in student members,
close to 300, and its participation as sponsor or co-sponsor of many ideas was
becoming impressive. Instead of putting on two or three programs each winter
month as it did during the 1940s, the club sometimes scheduled two or three
events a day in the 1970s. What with festivals and so-called extras and special
affairs, the seven-month schedule was often extended to a year-round operation.
Although the Schubert Club's major emphasis has always remained on performance and education, it also had time for slide shows, a number of film festivals,
vocal and piano music, and music of the Far East and Latin America, plus a
whole gaggle of new and experimental programs and musical get-togethers. A
boys' choir was also a child of the 1970s and very active for some years. In
1975, for example, it gave a total of seventy-five public performances. At the
end of the 1980-81 season, however, its activities were ended.

The first year in the 1970 decade was an especially important one for
the Schubert Club because it signaled a number of changes. The Artists'
Course, for example, was renamed International Artist Series, and a new recital
hall was first used. O'Shaughnessy Auditorium on the campus of the College
of St. Catherine in St. Paul was to be finished and available the first of the year.
Such, however, was not to be the case, and pianist Rudolf Firkusny returned
to St. Paul for the third time to give his February recital in the rather inade-
quate Central Presbyterian Church at Cedar and Exchange streets, St. Paul.
The acoustics were not good and the soloist suffered. And violinist Itzhak
Perlman, whose concert closed the season in a "blaze of glory," found that
the complicated series of steps and passages leading to the church's podium
made navigation far from easy for one on crutches.

When the first concert in the large new 1,700-seat O'Shaughnessy
Auditorium took place on October 19, 1970, soprano Beverly Sills made her
local recital debut before a jam-packed house. Music critic Allan Holbert reported in the *Minneapolis Tribune* that Sills "has to be one of the most charming singers ever to stand beside a grand piano." This concert began the Schubert Club's nine-year love affair with the New York Opera star who during
that short period performed before the group four different times ("Each
time is happy," Sills said.). Only three other musicians have equaled that
many repeats, but more on that later. Furthermore, all Sills's concerts were
sellouts. Her appearance in St. Paul on her farewell tour in 1979 bordered on
the clamorous, and club director Carlson said that he "could have sold out
Met Stadium." David Hawley, the new critic on the *Pioneer Press* who replaced
the retired Harvey, stated that, though hampered by laryngitis, she "earned
her standing ovation, but it was a disappointing victory — style and grace under
fire." By the end of 1970 the Schubert Club was well established in its new
concert hall. For the first time, to the regret of many, this change from the
Auditorium Theater took the recitals out of downtown St. Paul, for eighty-
eight years its habitat, and into the city's residential area. Beginning in 1984-

85, however, the International Series will once again return to the city's center upon the completion of the Ordway Music Theater facing Rice Park.

A connection with the Walker Art Center of Minneapolis also began early in the decade. At first the two organizations concentrated on the unusual and avant-garde with a series of contemporary concerts entitled "Nobody's Old Favorites" and with such programs as the "Noncert" of 1971. A year later they sponsored an Underwater recital at the Midway YMCA on New Year's Eve, 1972. On that occasion Texan Max Neuhaus, wearing flippers and swim trunks, created what some rapt listeners insisted were tones by pumping air and water through hoses attached to whistles submerged in the pool. In 1980 Neuhaus, a leader in the new school of environmental noises, returned to present another co-sponsored event using 64 loudspeakers scattered around the botanical gardens of the Como Conservatory in St. Paul. This installation was inaugurated with a champagne reception and a talk by St. Paul Mayor George Latimer. In 1983 the Neuhaus installation was removed from the Como Conservatory and refitted into the new museum building at Augsburg College. The employees of the Como Conservatory had not become fond of electronic music and were anxious for the change.

The fruitful alliance with Walker was not all avant-garde, however. The two groups also offered traditional concerts such as the distinguished – and popular –-Chamber Music Series. Throughout its long history, the Schubert Club has made special efforts to bring the small ensemble to St. Paul, for which it has received just praise. The first of the Schubert-Walker Chamber Music Series did not begin until the 1978-79 season, but the sponsors have since offered twenty-three outstanding performances by various distinguished small combinations. The favorite, the Juilliard String Quartet, has returned to St. Paul five times to perform at the Janet Wallace Fine Arts Center, Macalester College. In the January 13, 1971, issue of the *Pioneer Press*, critic Harvey characterized the Schubert Club as "Janus-headed . . . with a benevolent gaze on tradition and a lively interest in the present." No description could better fit the results of these cooperative efforts between the Schubert Club and Walker Art Center.

Almost seventy-five years ago the national magazine *Musical America* said of the Schubert Club that "the conviction is strong . . . that [it] has work to do in a field peculiarly its own"– a statement as true today as it was in 1909. During the mid-1970s the directors of this "Janus-headed" organization decided that commissioning works of music was also a field that should be actively pursued. One of the first such commissions was a fortuitous one. Dominick Argento of Minneapolis composed the song cycle *From the Diary of Virginia Woolf*, a major work which had its well-received premiere performance on January 5, 1975, at Orchestra Hall in Minneapolis. It was interpreted by the warm, rich voice of the English mezzo-soprano Janet Baker. Providing one of the high points in Schubert Club history, this first commissioned work went all the way to the top to win the Pulitzer Prize for music in 1975. Such encouragement led the club to do more commissioning. In April, 1979, another of Minnesota's leading composers, Libby Larsen, wrote a children's opera, *The Silver Fox*, at the request of the Schubert Club. In addition, a total of twelve works have been commissioned to honor the club's centennial season,

including compositions by Stephen Paulus, Paul Fetler, Stanislaw Skrowaczewski, Joan Tower, and other important composers. The club's interest in new
music has been reflected too, in the fact that the Minnesota Composers Forum,
an association of over 100 Minnesota composers, maintained office space within the Schubert Club offices from 1976 to 1983.

Only ten years after the Schubert Club thought it had found what
would finally be its permanent home, the organization had to decamp, aban-
doning its new quarters in the Arts and Science Center because of overcrowd-
ing and space limitations. The club was the first agency to move its phones,
files, and desks into the Old Federal Courts Building on Rice Park. That was
in 1974 when renovation work on the building had already been in progress
for almost a year. When the basic electrical, heating, plumbing and structural
phase of work had to begin, the Schubert Club once again was forced out
and from 1976 to 1978 took up quarters on the second and eighth floors of
the nearby St. Paul Building. Finally, during the summer of 1978, handsome
offices were re-established in the Federal Courts Building on the third floor,
southeast corner, overlooking the greenery and fountain of Rice Park, and
in full view of its future recital hall, the Ordway Music Theater. At 10 A.M.
on September 9, 1979, the old courthouse was reopened by Vice President
and Mrs. Walter F. Mondale and rededicated as the Landmark Center — the
magnificent new cultural headquarters in downtown St. Paul. Yet another
era had begun for the Schubert Club, this time in what is hoped will at last be
its permanent home.

The last decade of recitals in the International Artist Series had its
quota of fine artists. In 1974 and again in 1980 mezzo-soprano Marilyn Horne's
rich voice and superb artistry dazzled Schubert Club audiences, and the recitals
of soprano Victoria de los Angeles (1977) and of mezzo-soprano Frederica von
Stade (1979) were memorable. In addition, there were other superlative performances, one misunderstood recital, and a good concert hampered by what the
press called an "unpolite" audience. Seventy-seven-year-old Rudolf Serkin's
third appearance before the Schubert Club in March, 1980, left retired reviewer
Harvey at a loss for words: "one of the great experiences of many years of
concertgoing. . . words seem an impertinence." The third visit of pianist
Horowitz was first scheduled to coincide with his two St. Paul appearances in
March and October of 1928 — a 50th anniversary tour. Illness, however, de-
layed the performance seven months. The recital finally took place on Sunday
afternoon, May 20, 1979, in Orchestra Hall, Minneapolis, under the co-sponsorship of the Minnesota Orchestral Association and the St. Paul Schubert Club—
a helpful cooperative venture since the pianist received a $42,000 fee. The
sellout audience was delighted and wildly enthusiastic with what critic Hawley
of the *Pioneer Press* called Horowitz's "gloriously eccentric, freewheeling style."

In February, 1980, another concert presented a pleasant program of
early Renaissance music played on ancient instruments by the Waverly Consort.
It was, however, performed before a "lackadaisical audience." In fact, wrote
Gregory Peterson in the *Pioneer Press*, "many bolted from their seats without
even giving the performers an opportunity to take a bow." This "unpolite"
conduct was hardly condoned by the Schubert Club, but for such an intimate
program, perhaps the large O'Shaughnessy Auditorium mitigated against the

recital's success.

Finally, there was Alicia de Larrocha, one of the five artists in the club's hundred-year-history invited to return for a fourth time. Critic Harvey felt that "each visit . . . leaves treasured memories and each time she performs is a revelation of superlative pianism and interpretive art." De Larrocha's most recent appearance before the Schubert Club was in November, 1982, and like Beverly Sills, during her final recital in St. Paul in 1979, she was plagued by illness. An unfortunate, over-critical appraisal of the concert by a St. Paul reviewer notwithstanding, the Schubert Club's love affair with this outstanding artist has not cooled, according to director Carlson, "and our respect and sympathy for her have increased immensely."

Among the international artists who have appeared before the Schubert Club in its one hundred years, many recitalists have been engaged for second performances, but only eleven have made it back three times: pianists Adele Aus der Ohe, Harold Bauer, Rudolf Firkusny, Rudolf Serkin, and Gary Graffman; bass George London, baritone Heinrich Schlusnus, the Flonzaley Quartet, and the Kneisel, London, and Budapest String Quartets. Two other chamber music ensembles have returned to St. Paul for repeat recitals, but those were for the special yearly Chamber Music Series presented jointly by the Schubert Club and the Walker Art Center: the previously mentioned Juilliard String Quartet five times and the Guarneri String Quartet three times. In the International Artist Series, top honors for return performances have gone to only four soloists who over the years have been asked to come back to give four performances each before Schubert Club audiences: pianists Robert Casadesus and Alicia de Larrocha, violinist Isaac Stern (also a centennial performer), and soprano Beverly Sills.

A recent project of the Schubert Club, and one of its most rewarding, began in 1970 when it was given an 1830 Kisting piano, once played on by Clara Schumann and Brahms, and the idea was born for a museum of keyboard instruments which would reflect the history of Western musical art, serve as teaching aids, and add to the musical culture of the area. Under the leadership of the then club president, Mrs. Thomas F. Ellerbe, Jr., and the enthusiasm and energy of Bruce Carlson, plans moved slowly ahead until some half-hundred European and American pianos dating from the eighteenth and nineteenth centuries had been assembled through gift and purchase. The heart of the collection is the pianos of the early nineteenth century, yet the museum includes harpsichords, clavichords, and pianofortes of the eighteenth century and harpsichords of the seventeenth and sixteenth centuries with one exceptional instrument —a 1542 Annibale d'Rossi Italian spinet harpsichord —having the distinction of being the oldest keyboard instrument by a known maker in the United States. After ten years of planning and preparation, the museum opened on September 7, 1980, with a fortepiano recital given by Mary Briggs Sadovnikoff, herself a Schubert Club scholarship winner and daughter of the club's long-time member and major Twin Cities pianist Marjorie Winslow Briggs. Helen Hollis, from the Smithsonian Institution's musical instrument staff and primary consultant for the Schubert Club's collection, also came for the event. In an elaborate ceremony on November 30, 1981, the museum was dedicated to "Charlotte Ordway and her Schubert Club friends" because of the ongoing generosity of Charlotte Ordway's daughter, Mrs. Craig Wallace. Located in the lower level of the Landmark Center directly opposite the new Weyerhaeuser Auditorium, the imaginatively designed museum replaces the lunchroom used for many years by local postal workers. Philip Larson, Minneapolis sculptor and architectural designer, planned teh museum space and called it a Schatzkammer, or Treasure Room, which is exactly where antique instruments belong. In his words the room gives "the feeling of romantic seclusion — of a large security vault." Iron grates from the old elevator shafts in Landmark Center were refurbished into large gates which allow passersby to view the collection even when the museum is unattended. As part of a living museum, the instruments are displayed in rotation and are being played every day during the noon hour, to the delight of Landmark visitors. The first practical use in a major concert of these fine old instruments was in April, 1982, when Austrian pianist Jörg Demus — like Arnold Dolmetsch back in 1906, one of the leaders in the movement to perform early keyboard music on period instruments — used two of the pianos for his performance of works by Mozart, Beethoven, and Schubert. The Demus concert "was a treat," according to critic Roy M. Close in the *St. Paul Dispatch*, for the artist "matched his interpretation beautifully to the expressive powers of the instruments." Ten phonograph recordings have been pressed by the Schubert Club to honor its one hundred years. These include several by artists like Demus using pianos from the Schubert Club Keyboard Instrument Museum. Peter Serkin, too, recorded on the Schubert Club's splendid Graf piano bringing the museum to the attention of a front-rank artist.

Innovation and imagination have made the Schubert Club a national forerunner in the performing arts. The coming season of 1983-84 starts the second hundred years for the venerable Schubert Club, and its goals continue to be essentially what they were when first written and made public by Mrs. Russell Dorr in 1892: "To study and practice the best music. . . . To advance the interests and promote the culture of musical art in the City of St. Paul." After ninety years those aims are still being quietly followed with a large docket of civic activities. Today the club, though considerably expanded in its sphere of influence, still offers educational and financial aid and performing opportunities as well as vocational and instructional advantages for gifted music students and disadvantaged and minority pupils. The Schubert Club also provides a program of music therapy for the mentally retarded, physically handicapped, and elderly. The Master Classes, open to the public for a fee, give local musicians and students an opportunity to be exposed to the methodology and personalities of recognized artists such as baritone Gerard Souzay, flutist Jean-Pierre Rampal, pianist Rosalyn Tureck, the Danish baritone Aksel Schiøtz, soprano Phyllis Curtin, and many others. The Schubert Club is indeed an unabashed success story with many facets.

But it is the evening concerts, the International Artist Series, that continue to be their most prominent enterprises, as they were when the first recital season began in 1893 — the most daring, most expensive, and riskiest! A Sunday issue of the *Pioneer Press* back in November, 1901, lauded the women for attempting so many forms of musical work and achieving "such success in all directions." Just two years later Florence Briggs, then the club's new president, spoke (as previously mentioned) of the organization's "pride in its past" — in

1903 it had just reached its majority! She especially boasted of the "natural faith" the group had in its future. Little did they then know, and little could they have even guessed, where that faith in the future might lead them. On the Schubert Club's hundredth birthday, the optimism of seventy-nine years ago has been more than vindicated. During the hundredth year celebration all five of the International Artist Series Concerts were partially endowed, in perpetuity, by members of the St. Paul families long associated with the Schubert Club. These include Catherine M. Davis, Edward Brooks, Jr., Catherine and John Neimeyer by Nancy and Ted Weyerhaeuser, Reine H. Myers by the John H. Myers, Paul M. Myers Jr., and John Parrish families, and Charlotte Ordway by her children. And a substantial Visiting Artist Fund was begun by several Schubert Club supporters as well as an Education Fund established by the O'Shaughnessy Foundation.

There can be little doubt that the Schubert Club will continue to have a dedicated "natural faith in its future" for what undoubtedly will be a fascinating and fruitful second century.

APPENDICES

PROMINENT PERFORMING ARTISTS PRESENTED BY THE SCHUBERT CLUB (1882-1982)

Aguilar Lute Quartet, 1930
Alcock, Merle (contralto), 1921
Alexander, Arthur (tenor), 1919
Alvin Ailey American Dance Theater, 1969
Anievas, Agustin (pianist), 1970
Antoine, Josephine (soprano), 1940
Arnelle, Vernon d' (baritone), 1914
Arrau, Claudio (pianist), 1953
Ashkenazy, Vladimir (pianist), 1962, 1974
Aus der Ohe, Adèle (pianist), 1893, 1895,
    1904
Austin, Florence Muriel (violinist), 1909
Austral, Florence (soprano), 1929
Averino, Olga (soprano), 1932
Ax, Emanuel (pianist), 1983

Bach Aria Group, 1965, 1971
Bach Collegium and Kantorei Stuttgart, 1968
Bachauer, Gina (pianist), 1952, 1955
Badura-Skoda, Paul (pianist), 1954
Bailey-Apfelbeck, Marie Louise (pianist), 1923
Baker, Janet (mezzo-soprano), 1975, 1982
Bampton, Rose (contralto), 1933, 1946
Bannerman, Lois (harpist), 1946
Barrère Ensemble, 1951
Barromeo, Chase (baritone), 1935
Bartlett and Robertson (duo-pianists), 1930,
    1945
Bauer, Harold (pianist), 1925, 1930, 1939
Beach, John Parsons (pianist), 1898
Beethoven String Quartet, 1894
Bel Canto Trio, 1947, 1955
Bergh, Arthur (violinist), 1902, 1904
Berman, Lazar (pianist), 1979
Bispham, David (baritone), 1900
Blauvelt, Lillian (soprano), 1894
Bliss, Mr. and Mrs. James A. (duo-pianists),
    1922
Blye, Birdice (pianist), 1909
Bolet, Jorge (pianist), 1972
Bomar, Ann (mezzo-soprano), 1949
Bonelli, Richard (baritone), 1931
Bori, Lucrezia (soprano), 1922
Brailowsky, Alexander (pianist), 1938
Braslau, Sophie (contralto), 1915
Bream, Julian (guitarist, lutist), 1971, 1974
Brendel, Alfred (pianist), 1977, 1979
Breton, Ruth (violinist), 1924
Brown, Anne (soprano), 1943

Browning, John (pianist), 1965
Budapest String Quartet, 1941,
    1943 (twice)
Buswell, James Oliver IV (violinist), 1971

Casadesus, Robert (pianist), 1939, 1946,
    1963
Casadesus, Robert and Gaby (duo-pianists),
    1949
Cassado, Gasper (cellist), 1937
Chamber Music Society of Lincoln Center,
    1976
Chamlee, Mario (tenor), 1926
Chase, Mary Wood (pianist), 1906
Cherkassky, Shura (pianist), 1936
Chicago Symphony Orchestra, Theodore
    Thomas, conductor, 1900
Chilson-Ohrman, Luella (soprano), 1912
Clark, Charles W. (baritone), 1912
Collins, Edward (pianist), 1901, 1913
Collins, Robert Hall (baritone), 1947
Concentus Musicus, Vienna, 1978
Coolidge String Quartet, 1938, 1939
Corigliano, John (violinist), 1925
Cortez, Leonora (pianist), 1928
Cortot, Alfred (pianist), 1923, 1926
Cottlow, Augusta (pianist), 1909
Crooks, Richard (tenor), 1924, 1940
Culp, Julia (contralto), 1914
Curtin, Phyllis (soprano), 1968
Curzon, Clifford (pianist), 1949, 1955

Davidovich, Bella (pianist), 1981
Davies, David Thomas Ffrangcon-
    (baritone), 1899
Davis, Ellabelle (soprano), 1953
DeGogorza, Emilio (baritone), 1915
De Larrocha, Alicia (pianist), 1969, 1973,
    1977, 1982
De los Angeles, Victoria (soprano), 1977
Demus, Jörg (pianist), 1982
Dobbs, Mattiwilda (soprano), 1955
Doe, Doris (contralto), 1935
Dolmetsch, Arnold (ancient instruments),
    1906
Don Cossack Chorus, 1944
Duncan, Todd (baritone), 1944
Dux, Claire (soprano), 1924

Lachaume, Aimé (pianist), 1894, 1895
Lanzo, Mario (tenor), 1947
Laredo, Ruth (pianist), 1976
Lashanska, Hulda (soprano), 1920
Lateiner, Jacob (pianist), 1956
Lear, Evelyn (soprano), 1969
Leginska, Ethel (pianist), 1906
Lehmann, Lotte (soprano), 1936
Leider, Frida (soprano), 1931
Letz Quartet, 1924
Liege String Quartet, 1933
José Limon and Dance Company, 1961
Lindsay, William (pianist), 1922
Linne, Range (soprano), 1896
Lipp, Wilma (soprano), 1953
List, Eugene (pianist), 1947, 1950
Little Singers of Paris, 1957
Lloyd, David (tenor), 1956
Loewenguth Quartet, 1952
London, George (bass), 1947, 1951, 1960
London String Quartet, 1923, 1927, 1950
Lull, Barbara (violinist), 1928

Carmelita Maracci Dance Group, 1941
Marchesi, Blanche (soprano), 1899
Mario, Queena (soprano), 1925
Marlboro Festival Quintet, 1974
Marshall, Lois (soprano), 1959
Marteau, Henri (violinist), 1894, 1898
Masselos, William (pianist), 1962
Melton, James (tenor), 1942
Menges, Isolde (violinist), 1919
Méro, Yolanda (pianist), 1921
Miles, Gwilym (baritone), 1904
Miller, Christine (contralto), 1908 (twice)
Miller, Ruth (soprano), 1926
Milstein, Nathan (violinist), 1958
Minneapolis Symphony Orchestra, 1906
Minneapolis Symphony Quartette, 1912,
     1919
Moiseiwitsch, Benno (pianist), 1921,
     1949
Moon, Ick Choo (pianist), 1978
Morgan, Geraldine (violinist), 1893
Morini, Erica (violinist), 1950
Mortimer, Myra (contralto), 1927
Moscow Chamber Orchestra, 1966
Mundy, Anne (pianist), 1936
Muzio, Claudia (soprano), 1927

Netherlands Chamber Orchestra, 1961
Netherlands String Quartet, 1960
New York Chamber Soloists, 1964
New York Pro Musica, 1973
New York Quartet, 1953

New York String Quartet, 1928
Nicholson, Robert (baritone), 1940
Niemack, Ilse (violinist), 1927
Nikolaidi, Elena (contralto), 1950
Norman, Jessye (soprano), 1976
Novaes, Guiomar (pianist), 1953, 1968

Olszewska, Maria (contralto), 1928
Orloff, Nikolai (pianist), 1926, 1928
Orpheus Quartet, 1902
Orth, Peter (pianist), 1980

Paganini Quartet, 1948
Paratore, Anthony and Joseph
     (pianists), 1979
Paur, Emil (pianist), 1905
Pelton-Jones, Frances (harpsichordist),
     1920
Perabo, Ernest (pianist), 1895
Perlman, Itzhak (violinist), 1970, 1980
Perry, Edward Baxter, (pianist), 1893
Peterson, Edna Gunnar (pianist), 1916
Piatigorsky, Gregor (cellist), 1931
Price, Leontyne (soprano), 1961

Quartetto Italiano, 1953

Rampal, Jean-Pierre (flutist), 1981
Renard, Rosita (pianist), 1920
Renardy, Ossy (violinist), 1937
Rethbergh, Elisabeth (soprano), 1927
Ricci, Ruggiero (violinist), 1962
Richter-Haaser, Hans (pianist), 1960
Riedelsberger String Quartette, 1901
Ringen, Jessie M. (contralto), 1905
Robinson, Carol (pianist), 1919
Rose, Leonard (cellist), 1956, 1973
Rosenthal, Moriz (pianist), 1899
Rostropovich, Mstislav (cellist),
     1963, 1981
Roth Quartet, 1929
Royal Uppsala University Chorus of
     Sweden, 1970
Edith Rubel Trio, 1917
Rubenstein, Artur (pianist), 1942
Rubinstein String Quartet, 1893,
     1894

St. Paul Choral Art Society, 1910, 1914
St. Paul Symphony Orchestra, 1912
St. Paul Symphony Woodwind Quintette,
     1911

Samaroff, Olga (pianist), 1924
Sauer, Emil (pianist), 1899
Sayao, Bidu (soprano), 1939, 1945
Schaaf, Peter (pianist), 1966
Scharwenka, Xaver (pianist), 1894
Schelling, Ernest (pianist), 1917
Schevill, Clara M. (contralto), 1929
Schickele, Peter (P.D.Q. Bach - comic),
    1967, 1982
Schipa, Tito (tenor), 1926
Schlusnus, Heinrich (baritone), 1927,
    1929, 1933
Schub, André-Michel (pianist), 1979
Schwartz, Joseph (baritone), 1923
Schwarzkopf, Elisabeth (soprano),
    1954
Seefried, Irmgard (soprano), 1952,
    1958
Seidel, Toscha (violinist), 1922
Serkin, Peter (pianist), 1969
Serkin, Rudolf (pianist), 1961, 1977,
    1980
Shafran, Daniel (cellist), 1978
Sharnova, Sonia (contralto), 1932
Shattuck, Arthur (pianist), 1918
Sherman, Blanche (pianist), 1904
Sherwood, William H. (pianist), 1893
Shure, Leonard (pianist), 1944
Silber, Sidney J. (pianist), 1906
Sills, Beverly (soprano), 1970, 1972,
    1975, 1979
Singher, Martial (baritone), 1948
Smeterlin, Jan (pianist), 1931, 1933
Societa Corelli, 1956
Solisti de Zagreb, 1957, 1960
Solomon (pianist), 1951
Southwick, Frederick (baritone), 1920
Souzay, Gérard (baritone), 1952, 1964
Spalding, Albert (violinist), 1931
Spivakov, Vladimir (violinist), 1978
Spivakovsky, Tossy (violinist), 1948
Sprotte, Berthold (contralto), 1909
Steber, Eleanor (soprano), 1943
Stein, Gertrude May (soprano), 1898
Stephens, Clyde (pianist), 1923
Stern, Isaac (violinist), 1943, 1947, 1951,
    1983
Stewart, Reginald (pianist), 1942
Stoltzman, Richard (clarinetist), 1982
Stradivarius Quartet, 1935
Strong, May Fairfield (pianist), 1900
Stueckgold, Grete (soprano), 1932
Swedish Radio Choir, 1974
Szeryng, Henry (violinist), 1934, 1940
Szigeti, Joseph (violinist), 1965

Talvela, Martti (bass), 1978
Thebom, Blanche (soprano), 1946
Thomas, John Charles (baritone), 1930,
    1937
Tinayre, Yves (tenor), 1942
Traubel, Helen (soprano), 1938, 1948
Travers, Patricia (violinist), 1944
Trio Aeolienne, 1920
Trio de Lutece, 1916
Tureck, Rosalyn (pianist), 1966

Valente, Benita (soprano), 1971
Valletti, Cesare (tenor), 1962
Varnay, Astrid (soprano), 1945
Verrett, Shirley (mezzo-soprano), 1964
Vienna Octet, 1958
Virtuosi de Roma, 1964
Vishnevskaya, Galina (soprano), 1967
von Stade, Frederica (mezzo-soprano),
    1979
VonWarlich, Reinhold (bass), 1900,
    1910
Vreeland, Jeanette (soprano), 1931
Vronsky and Babin (duo-pianists),
    1946

Roger Wagner Chorale, 1963, 1965
Waverly Consort, 1980
Weissgerber, Andreas (violinist), 1932
Werrenrath, Reinald (baritone), 1917
Wilson, Genevieve Clark (soprano),
    1897
Winters, Lawrence (baritone), 1953
Witherspoon, Herbert (bass), 1904,
    1909
Wysor, Elizabeth (contralto), 1940

Yaw, Ellen Beach (soprano), 1894
Yeend, Frances (soprano), 1947
Ysäye, Eugene (violinist), 1895

Zeisler, Fannie Bloomfield (pianist),
    1901, 1911
Zoellner String Quartet, 1918
Zukerman, Pinchas and Eugenia
    (violinist and flutist), 1975
Zukerman, Pinchas (violinist), 1981

PRESIDENTS OF THE SCHUBERT CLUB

Mrs. Charles McIlrath 1882-1886
Mrs. Charles E. Furness 1886-1887
Mrs. Harcourt H. Horn 1887-1888
Mrs. Lyman D. Hodge. 1888-1892
Mrs. Russell R. Dorr 1892-1900
Miss Elsie M. Shawe 1900-1902
Mrs. Warren S. Briggs 1902-1905
Miss Gertrude E. Hall 1905-1908
Mrs. Warren S. Briggs 1908-1930
Mrs. Charles A. Guyer. 1930-1933
Mrs. Webb R. Raudenbush 1933-1943
Mrs. Juilian S. Gilman 1943-1948
Mrs. John C. Neimeyer 1948-1951
Mrs. Charles E. Porter. 1951-1954
Mrs. Charles H. Loomis 1954-1957
Mrs. Seigel A. Anderson. 1957-1959
Mrs. William H. Abbott 1959-1961
Mrs. S. Axel von Bergen 1961-1963
Mrs. Knight Pryor 1963-1965
Mrs. Leonard G. Olson 1965-1967
Mrs. Kenneth O. Johnson 1967-1969
Mrs. Henry Kartarik 1969-1971
Mrs. Thomas F. Ellerbe, Jr. 1971-1973
Mrs. John A. McNeill 1973-1975
Mrs. Gordon Shepard 1975-1979
Mrs. Donald Sell 1979-1983
Mrs. John Diehl 1983-

ACKNOWLEDGMENTS

The Schubert Club Papers can be found at both the Minnesota Historical Society and at the club's headquarters in the Landmark Center, St. Paul. The former holds most of the material through 1966, including several manuscript club histories of varying length: by Mrs. Simon P. Crosby (1901); by Henrietta W. Willius (1915); by Mrs. Clifford L. Hilton (1923); one probably by Mrs. Charles A. Guyer about 1931; and by Zylpha S. Morton (1962), a portion of which was issued by the club in mimeographed form in 1964. In addition, information concerning concerts, lectures, etc., has come from minutes, committee reports, and a series of scrapbooks which are a part of the Schubert Club Papers, or from a chronologically arranged collection of programs in the Library of the Minnesota Historical Society. That library also has a file of informal reports, or *Yearbooks* published annually by the club.

I am especially grateful for the careful and detailed research of the 1882-1940 period compiled by John Schwiebert in 1981 which has added much information and helped clear up a number of problems. Also of use was the material on the 1940-1980 period gathered by Mrs. Robert Bowen, daughter of St. Paul violinist Margaret Horn Russell. Both these lengthy manuscripts can be found among the Schubert Club Papers at the Minnesota Historical Society and at the Schubert Club headquarters. Special thanks also due the Schubert Club and its Executive Director Bruce P. Carlson for help and encouragement, to an editorial committee comprised of John Harvey, Mary Ann Feldman and Russell Fridley for readings of the research material and various manuscripts, to Sharon M. Carlson for production assistance, as well as to my co-workers John A. Dougherty, Robert E. Hoag, Dallas Lindgren, Bonnie Wilson, and Patricia Harpole of the State Historical Society staff. Nine photographs were also used by permission from the Minnesota Historical Society (the balance of the photographs are from the Schubert Club's own archives and collection). Above all, gratitude goes to the senior editor at the Historical Society, Kenneth A. Carley, former editor of *Minnesota History,* for his critical reading of the manuscript and for his deft editorial work.

— *James Taylor Dunn*